Illustrator
Ken Tunell

Editor
Barbara M. Wally, M.S.

Editorial Project Manager
Ina Massler Levin, M.A.

Editor in Chief
Sharon Coan, M.S. Ed.

Art Director
Elayne Roberts

Associate Designer
Denise Bauer

Cover Artist
Larry Bauer

Product Manager
Phil Garcia

Imaging
David Bennett
Ralph Olmedo, Jr.

Researcher
Christine Johnson

Publishers
Rachelle Cracchiolo, M.S. Ed.
Mary Dupuy Smith, M.S. Ed.

The Twenties

Author

Mary Ellen Sterling, M.Ed.

Teacher Created Materials, Inc.
6421 Industry Way
Westminster, CA 92683
www.teachercreated.com
©*1996 Teacher Created Materials, Inc.*
Reprinted, 2000
Made in U.S.A.
ISBN-1-57690-024-X

Table of Contents

Table of Contents *(cont.)*

Introduction

The 20th Century is a series which examines the political, economic, social, cultural, scientific, and technological advances of the twentieth century and introduces students to the individuals who made history in each decade.

The Twenties chronicles a decade of dramatic change. In the wake of World War I, the focus of America was inward. For the first time immigrants were not welcomed. America was changing from its pre-war, rural economy into an urban, industrial nation. Innovations and inventions flourished, changing almost every aspect of American life. Affordable automobiles changed the landscape, and radio and films brought culture and politics to everyone. Many advanced technologies, like television, computers, and space travel, have roots in the 20s.

It was a glittering time of flappers, parties, and frivolous fads. Jazz, a new and uniquely American sound, became popular. Women won the vote in time for the election of 1920. With it came a new sense of equality. They raised their hemlines, bobbed their hair, went to college, and joined the work force. Prohibition, accepted in theory, was openly flouted. Speakeasies opened by the thousands, and hip flasks were common accessories. While citizens defied the law, organized crime flourished as bootlegging became big business.

The stock market spiralled upward, driven by the market for durable goods and by master manipulators. Once the realm of the rich, people from all levels of society entered the market, buying on small margins. Some, like President Hoover, believed that the prosperity would last forever. But the euphoria and the decade ended on October 29, 1929, with the crash of the stock market and the dawn of the Great Depression.

The Twenties profiles the presidents who shaped the decade, the heroes like Charles Lindbergh and Babe Ruth who earned a place in history, the writers and artists who captured the spirit of the times, and the inventors and innovators who changed the world.

This unit includes

- ❑ a time line—a chronology of significant events of the decade
- ❑ planning guides—summaries and suggested activities for introducing the key issues and events of the decade
- ❑ personality profiles—brief biographies of important individuals of the decade
- ❑ a chronology of world events—a list of individuals and events in other countries during this decade
- ❑ language experience ideas—suggestions for writing and vocabulary building
- ❑ group activities—assignments to foster cooperative learning
- ❑ topics for further research—suggestions for extending the unit
- ❑ literature connections—summaries of related books and suggested activities for expanding them.
- ❑ curriculum connections—activities in math, art, language arts, social studies, and music
- ❑ computer applications—suggestions for selecting and using software to supplement this unit
- ❑ a bibliography—suggestions for additional resources on the decade

To keep this valuable resource intact so that it can be used year after year, you may wish to punch holes in the pages and store them in a three-ring binder.

Time Line

	1920	1921
Politics and Economics	President: Thomas Woodrow Wilson Vice-President: Thomas Riley Marshall President Wilson asks voters to endorse the League of Nations. On August 18 The Nineteenth Amendment is ratified, giving women the right to vote. The Merchant Marine Act is passed. The Prohibition Amendment becomes law. The ACLU is founded.	President: Warren Gamaliel Harding Vice-President: John Calvin Coolidge Armistice Day is declared a legal holiday. The Federal Highway Act is signed into law. Congress halts immigration with tough quota laws. Mrs. W. H. Felton of Georgia becomes the first woman in the U.S. Senate. President Harding pardons Eugene V. Debs, convicted of violating the 1917 Espionage Act.
Social and Cultural	African Americans form baseball's Negro National League. Bill Tilden is the first American to win Wimbledon. Babe Ruth is sold to the Yankees for $125,000. The first radio station—KDKA Pittsburgh—begins broadcasting.	Margaret Sanger helps found the American Birth Control League. Margaret Gorman wins the first Miss America pageant. Betty Crocker is invented to represent the Washburn Crosby Company. Sacco and Vanzetti are tried and convicted.
Science and Technology	The first hair dryer is introduced. Earle Dickson invents the Band-Aid.	Einstein wins the Nobel Prize for Physics for his theory of relativity. Insulin is first used to treat diabetes.

Time Line (cont.)

1922	1923	1924
The Washington Conference ends the naval arms race.	President Harding dies; Coolidge is sworn in as president.	Calvin Coolidge is elected President.
Albert Fall gives Mammoth Oil Company the rights to Teapot Dome oil reserves.	The Teapot Dome scandal comes to light.	Miriam Ferguson of Texas and Nellie Ross of Wyoming are elected governors on the same day.
		The U.S. grants full citizenship to Native Americans.
		J. Edgar Hoover is appointed director of the FBI.
T.S. Eliot writes *The Wasteland*.	The Charleston (a dance) is introduced.	George Gershwin composes *Rhapsody in Blue*.
The bestselling book is a book about manners by Emily Post.	Tutmania sweeps the country; Egyptian colors and scarab jewelry are fashionable.	The first winter Olympics are held in France.
Reader's Digest is first published.	The first blues recording is made by Bessie Smith.	Membership in the KKK is at an all-time high.
Peanut butter and jelly sandwiches become popular.	The KKK actively terrorizes Blacks and Native Americans.	Bigfoot is sighted.
Annie Oakley breaks sharpshooting records.	Yankee Stadium is built.	The dance marathon is the new craze in America; the record for nonstop dancing is 90 hours.
Bessie Coleman becomes the nation's first female internationally licensed pilot.		Saks Fifth Avenue opens.
Johnny Weissmuller swims 100 meters in under one minute.		
Dr. Alexis Carrel discovers white corpuscles in the blood.	The electric shaver is patented.	Kimberly Clark introduces Kleenex.
B.A. Fiske builds the first microfilm machine.	Vladimir Zworykin obtains the first patent on the television tube.	The first contact lenses are imported.
	Garrett A. Morgan receives a patent for the three-way automatic electric stoplight.	Edwin Hubble announces the discovery of other galaxies in the universe.

6

Time Line (cont.)

1925	1926	1927
President: Calvin Coolidge is inaugurated. Vice President: Charles Gates Dawes The Scopes Trial tests a Tennessee law that bans teaching evolution. Nellie Ross of Wyoming takes office as the first female governor in the U.S.	The Civil Aviation Act is passed.	Coolidge sends 5,000 U.S. Marines to Nicaragua.
The Great Gatsby by F. Scott Fitzgerald is published. *Winnie the Pooh* books are first published. The first motel opens in California. Florida land speculation peaks. The first national spelling bee is held.	The heartthrob actor Rudolph Valentino dies. The entertainer and magician Harry Houdini dies. The impressionist artist Mary Cassatt dies. Gertrude Ederle becomes the first woman to swim the English Channel. NBC is formed. Richard E. Byrd successfully flies over the North Pole. Charlie Chaplin stars in *The Gold Rush.* Cars are painted in colors for the first time. The Book-of-the-Month Club begins.	Charles Lindbergh makes the first solo flight across the Atlantic. Babe Ruth hits a record 60 home runs in one season. CBS is established. Gutzon Borglum begins carving Mt. Rushmore. The first talking movie, *The Jazz Singer* starring Al Jolson, is exhibited. Ford introduces the Model A car. Yo-yos are first imported from the Philippines.
Dry ice is first manufactured. Potato chips are first manufactured.	The first pop-up toaster is patented. R. H. Goddard launches the first successful liquid-fueled rocket.	Rice Krispies make their debut on the market. The Baby Ruth candy bar is invented. The Epsicle, later renamed the Popsicle, is invented. Patent leather shoes are introduced.

Time Line *(cont.)*

	Politics and Economics	Social and Cultural	Science and Technology
1929	President: Herbert Clark Hoover is inaugurated as the thirty-first President. Vice President: Charles Curtis The stock market crashes on October 29.	The first science-fiction comic strip is introduced—*Buck Rogers*. The first Oscars are presented. Construction is begun on the Empire State Building. Al Capone's mob shoots down rival mobsters in Chicago's St. Valentine's Day Massacre. Legend and lawman Wyatt Earp dies at the age of 80.	Clarence Birdseye develops frozen vegetables. Kodak produces the first 16mm color photographic film.
1928	Coolidge decides not to run for reelection. Fifteen countries accept the Kellogg-Briand Act which outlaws war. Herbert Hoover beats Al Smith in the presidential election.	Amelia Earhart becomes the first woman to fly across the Atlantic. Walt Disney produces the first animated cartoon with sound, *Steamboat Willie*. Laurel and Hardy are popular at the box office. Fifteen-year-old Sonia Henie wins a gold medal in ice skating at the Olympics.	Alexander Fleming discovers penicillin. George Eastman invents the first colored motion pictures. The iron lung is used to treat polio.

Using the Time Line

Use pages five to eight to create a visual display for your classroom. Follow the steps outlined below to assemble the time line as a bulletin board display and then choose from the suggested uses those that best suit your classroom needs.

Bulletin Board Assembly

Copy pages five to eight. Enlarge and/or color them, if desired. Tape the pages together to form a continuous time line and attach it to a prepared bulletin board background or a classroom wall. (To make a reusable bulletin board, glue each page of the time line to oaktag. After the pages have dried, laminate them. Write on the laminated pages with dry erase markers.)

Time Line

	1920	1921	1922	1923	1924	1925	1926	1927	1928	1929	
Politics and Economics	President: Thomas Woodrow Wilson. Vice-President: Thomas Riley Marshall. President Wilson asks voters to endorse the League of Nations. On August 18 the Nineteenth Amendment is ratified, giving women the right to vote. The Merchant Marine Act is passed. The Prohibition Amendment becomes law. The ACLU is founded.	President: Warren Gamaliel Harding. Vice-President: John Calvin Coolidge. Armistice Day is declared a legal holiday. The Federal Highway Act is signed into law. Congress halts immigration with tough quota laws. Mrs. W. H. Felton of Georgia becomes the first woman in the U.S. Senate. President Harding pardons Eugene V. Debs, convicted of violating the 1917 Espionage Act.	The Washington Conference ends the naval arms race. Americans grow disenchanted with Prohibition. The Teapot Dome scandal comes to light.	President Harding dies, Coolidge is sworn in as president. The Teapot Dome scandal comes to light.	Calvin Coolidge is elected President. White emigrant of Texas and Nellie Ross of Wyoming are elected governors for the same day. The U.S. grants full citizenship to Native Americans. J. Edgar Hoover is appointed director of the FBI.	President Calvin Coolidge is inaugurated. Vice-President: Charles Gates Dawes. The Scopes Trial tests a Tennessee law that bars teaching evolution. Nellie Ross of Wyoming takes office as the first female governor in the U.S.	The Civil Aviation Act is passed.	Coolidge sends 5,000 U.S. Marines to Nicaragua.	Coolidge decides not to run for reelection. Fifteen nations accept the Kellogg-Briand Act which outlaws war. Herbert Hoover beats Al Smith in the presidential election.	President: Herbert Clark Hoover is inaugurated as the thirty-first President. Vice-President: Charles Curtis. The stock market crashes on October 29.	**Politics and Economics**
Social and Cultural	African Americans form baseball's Negro National League. Bill Tilden is the first American to win Wimbledon. Babe Ruth is sold to the Yankees for $125,000. The first radio station—KDKA Pittsburgh—begins broadcasting.	Margaret Sanger helps found the American Birth Control League. Margaret Gorman wins the first Miss America pageant. Betty Crocker is invented to represent the Washburn Crosby Company. Sacco and Vanzetti are tried and convicted.	T.S. Eliot writes The Waste Land. The bestselling book is a best-seller of nurses by Emily Post. Reader's Digest is first published. Pearl buttons and jelly sandwiches become popular. Annie Oakley leads sharpshooting records. Jeanne Eagels becomes the actress's favorite intercultural licensed pilot. Johnny Weissmuller swims 100 meters in under one minute.	The Charleston is through & introduced. Vitamin escapes the counter, together colors and morals poetry on fashionable. Pearl buttons and jelly sandwiches become popular. The NBC actively becomes Bucks and Helen Hayes.	Greta Garbo rises to screen. Rhapsody in Blue. The first winter Olympics are held in France. Showboat by the 1926 is a hit and choose high. Hyde is sighted. The dance weathers its human rage in America, the second for teenage dancing is 87 hours. Babe Ruth hits many home runs.	The heartthrob actor Rudolph Valentino dies. The entertainer and magician Harry Houdini dies. The top-rated radio act is Amos 'n' Andy. Gertrude Ederle becomes the first woman to swim the English Channel. NBC is formed. Richard E. Byrd successfully flies over the North Pole. Charlie Chaplin stars in The Gold Rush. Cars are painted in colors for the first time. The Book-of-the-Month Club begins.	Charles Lindbergh makes the first solo flight across the Atlantic. Babe Ruth hits a record 60 home runs in one season. Golden Boy/Jane begins carving W. Rushmore. The first talking movie, The Jazz Singer starring Al Jolson, is exhibited. Floyd and speculation peaks.	Amelia Earhart becomes the first woman to fly across the Atlantic. Walt Disney produces the first animated cartoon with sound, Steamboat Willie. Laurel and Hardy are popular at the box office. Fifteen-year-old Sonja Henie wins a gold medal in ice skating at the Olympics.	The first science-fiction comic strip is introduced—Buck Rogers. The first Oscars are presented. Construction is begun on the Empire State Building. Al Capone's mob shoots down rival mobsters in Chicago's St. Valentine's Day Massacre. Legend and lawman Wyatt Earp dies at the age of 80.	**Social and Cultural**
Science and Technology	The first hair dryer is introduced. Earle Dickson invents the Band-Aid.	Einstein wins the Nobel Prize for Physics for his theory of relativity. Insulin is first used to treat diabetes.	Dr. Alexis Carrel discovers white corpuscles in the blood. H.K. Hales builds the first microfilm machine.	The electric shaver is patented. Insulin dramatically enters the body production for diabetes law. Garrett A. Morgan receives a patent for the three-way automatic electric stoplight.	Kimberly-Clark introduces Kleenex. The first contact lenses are reported. Edwin Hubble announces his discovery of other galaxies in the universe.	Dry ice is first manufactured. Potato chips are first manufactured.	The first pop-up toaster is patented. R.H. Goddard launches the first successful liquid fueled rocket.	Alexander Fleming discovers penicillin. George Eastman invents the first colored motion pictures. The iron lung is used to treat polio.	Clarence Birdseye develops frozen vegetables. Kodak produces the first 16mm color photographic film.	**Science and Technology**

Suggested Uses

1. Use the time line to assess students' initial knowledge of the era. Construct a web to find out what they know about the important events and individuals of the 1920s. Find out what they would like to know. Plan your lessons accordingly.

2. Assign each group of students a specific year. As they research that year, let them add pictures, names, and events to the appropriate area of the time line.

3. Assign students to find out what events were happening around the world during the 1920s. Tell them to add that information to the bottom of the time line.

4. After adding new names, places, and events to the time line, use the information gathered as a guide for assessment. Base your quizzes and exams on those people, places, and events that you have studied.

5. Have students research further some of the events and people listed on the time line. Reports can be presented orally or in a written format.

6. Use the time line as a springboard for class discussions—for example, Who was the most famous or influential person of the 1920s? What was Prohibition, and what would happen if that policy were instituted today? How was life in the 1920s similar to life today?

7. Divide the students into three groups and assign each group a different area: politics/economics, social/cultural, and science/technology. Have each group brainstorm important related people, places, and events that occurred during the twenties. Create a group mural depicting these important happenings. Get permission to decorate a hallway wall or tape several sheets of butcher paper together to make a giant canvas.

Twenties Overview

This overview provides a summary of important events that helped shape the twenties decade.

When Warren Harding campaigned for the presidency in 1920, he promised a "return to normalcy." For most Americans, this meant a return to life as it had been before World War I, but the war had changed America and the world too much. Harding's brief administration is remembered for its corruption, especially the Teapot Dome scandal. After Harding's untimely death in 1923, Calvin Coolidge was sworn into office. Believing that "The chief business of America is business," Coolidge shepherded tax laws through Congress that were mostly favorable to businesses. In 1928, Herbert Hoover, who promised "four years of prosperity," won the presidency by a landslide. After the stock market crash of 1929, Hoover was largely blamed for the disaster.

Prohibition became the law of the land in 1920. No one is certain whether drinking increased during Prohibition or not, but it did spread among women and youth and became a symbol of defiance. It also gave rise to organized crime and increased violence. Bootlegging was a big business.

By the end of the twenties almost every family had an automobile—a novelty at the beginning of the decade. Radios brought comedy shows and news nightly to families throughout the country and changed political campaigns. People flocked to the movies, and in 1927 they even had sound.

Musicians George Gershwin and Aaron Copland, writers Ernest Hemingway and F. Scott Fitzgerald, and artists Mary Cassatt and Grant Wood became prominent. In the predominantly Black populated section of Harlem in New York City, the Harlem Renaissance produced a host of great African American writers, artists, and musicians.

Fostered by presidents who favored business, the stock market reached new heights before the crash on October 29, 1929. At first President Hoover believed that the situation was temporary and refused to allow government aid for homeless and out-of-work people. His seeming insensitivity to the plight of the American people cost him the election of 1930.

For Discussion

1. What innovations were making their way into the everyday lives of the American people during the 1920s? How did these innovations change the lifestyles of the typical American?

2. Can you imagine your life now with only radio and no television? How would your life be different if that were the case?

3. Was it fair for the American public to blame Hoover for the effects of the stock market crash? How could this disaster possibly have been avoided?

4. What safety improvements have been made in the automobile since its invention? What problems has the automobile brought to our lives? How would your life be different without the automobile?

Introducing the 1920s

Here are a dozen interesting ways to introduce the 1920s. Try as many as you like. Modify them to suit your own classroom needs and teaching style.

1. Conduct discussion sessions as outlined on page 12, focusing on the 1920s.

2. Set up a special table with 1920s games and toys: Tinker Toys, Erector sets, checkers, crossword puzzles. Schedule times for groups of students to use the center.

3. Fill a jar with a mix of popular 1920s candies: licorice sticks, lollipops, Tootsie Rolls, jawbreakers. Have students estimate how many treats are in the jar. Award prizes for correct (or closest) answers.

4. In the twenties young people collected things like bottle caps and shiny foil gum and candy wrappers. With the class, brainstorm a list of everyday things they might collect. Let each student choose one to collect throughout your 1920s studies. On a specified day have students take turns sharing their collections.

5. Listen to some 1920s music from jazz to blues to popular tunes. If possible, enlist the help of the music teacher to teach students a twenties song. For arrangements and music, see *The Decade Series: Songs of the 20's* (Hal Leonard Publishing Corporation).

6. Provide groups of students with magazines and scissors. Direct the groups to cut out pictures of things and conveniences that they would not have found in the 1920s. Discuss and review all choices in whole group before creating a class collage.

7. Label a table with a handmade sign that says "Twenties Firsts." Display some items first invented or popularized during the 1920s, like Kleenex, Band-Aids, zippers, frozen foods (empty the package for display), Welch's grape jelly, Wrigley's chewing gum, and Eskimo Pies (the wrapper or empty box).

8. Advertising in the 1920s often made false claims about products because there were no laws governing these claims. Pair students and instruct them to choose an ad for any product in a magazine or newspaper. Tell them to rewrite the ad with exaggerated claims. Display the ads.

9. Playing with paper dolls was a popular pastime among girls in the twenties. Have students work in pairs to make life-size paper dolls. Spread a large sheet of butcher paper on the floor. One partner lies on the paper while the other partner traces around him/her with a black marking pen. Repeat the process for the other partner. Cut out the bodies and draw 1920s clothes on the life-size figures (encourage students to research twenties clothing for children). Display the paper dolls on the classroom walls.

10. Conduct a marathon. Divide the students into groups and let them plan a physical activity like jumping rope or calisthenics. See which group can go the longest nonstop.

11. Construct time capsules. Divide the students into small groups and use the methods and questionnaire on page 14. Work on this project for the remainder of the unit.

12. Bows for boys and girls were popular in the twenties. Make some ribbon or fabric bows to use as bow ties for boys and hair bows for girls. Designate a Bow Day when everyone wears his/her bow.

Discussing the Twenties

Create interest with a lively discussion. Suggested topics and methods follow.

Boys vs. Girls

Read aloud a description of flappers (a great source is *War, Peace, and All That Jazz* by Joy Hakim, (Oxford University Press, 1995). Have the boys and the girls respond to their respective questions.

Girls: If you had lived in the twenties, would you have become a flapper? Defend your answer. Do you think your parents would approve if you decided to be a flapper? What might be some of their objections?

Boys: If you were a boy during the twenties and your sister or girlfriend decided to be a flapper, how would you react? Would your parents approve of your having a girlfriend who is a flapper? Why or why not?

With the whole group discuss the girls' responses first and then the boys'. Extend the discussion by asking students to compare flappers to modern teenage groups. Brainstorm a list of similarities between teenagers of the twenties and teenagers today.

Modern Technology

Many appliances we take for granted today, like television and computers, did not exist in the 1920s. Ask the students to brainstorm some technologies that are available today and list them on the board or overhead projector. Discuss which of these technologies existed in the 1920s and circle them. Leave the list on display.

Write this statement and question on the board or overhead projector and give students time to think about them before proceeding with a discussion. During the 1920s the American lifestyle changed dramatically due to the advent of modern technology. What were some of these technologies? Add to your list any technologies not mentioned in the first part of this activity. Extend the lesson with this question: Can the same statement be applied to the current decade?

Imaginary Interviews

1. Ask the class to brainstorm a list of famous people from the 1920s or assign pairs to research a list of ten popular figures, along with their occupations. Two fine resources are *The 1920s* by Richard Tames (Franklin Watts, 1991) and *War, Peace, and All That Jazz* by Joy Hakim. List all names and occupations on the board or overhead projector.

2. Ask the students what they would like to ask these people about life in the twenties and record their responses on the board. Divide the class into pairs or small groups. Tell them to choose one figure and write an interview with that person. Questions and answers are to be included in their responses. Research for answers, if necessary. Have each pair share their interview with another pair.

Teacher's Note: For an interview form, see page 13.

A 1920s Interview

Here is a guide for you to use when interviewing your 1920s figure. Add any other questions you may have for this person. Remember to respond to the questions as the person you are interviewing.

Name _____

Date of Birth _____

Place of Birth _____

Occupation _____

1. Tell some things about your early childhood memories.

   _____

   _____

2. Explain what events in your childhood influenced your choice of career.

   _____

   _____

3. Who were some people who influenced your career?

   _____

   _____

4. What were some of the obstacles and struggles you encountered throughout your career? Explain how you overcame them.

   _____

   _____

   _____

   _____

5. What do you think you will be most remembered for after you are gone?

   _____

   _____

   _____

6. What would you like written as your epitaph? (Write this epitaph on the tombstone at the right.)

   _____

   _____

   _____

Twenties Time Capsule

It is the 1920s, and you and your friends want to preserve the times for future people your age.

Read and answer the following questions to determine what information to include in your time capsule. Cut pictures and articles from magazines and newspapers to represent twenties things, collect artifacts, and write stories and articles. Once you have your collection, use the suggestions below to decide how to freeze your memories.

What to Collect

1. What books do you like to read?

2. Who are some of your favorite movie actors? What movies have they appeared in? How much did you pay for your ticket to the movies? Which cartoon character is your favorite?

3. What are some brand new products on the market? How much do they cost?

4. What are some chores you have to do at home?

5. How much allowance do you receive? How do you spend this money?

6. What does your mother typically serve for dinner?

7. What types of snacks are available? How much do they cost?

8. What games do you like to play? What types of toys are available?

9. Who are some important people in the news these days? What has made them famous?

Ways to Freeze Memories

Paste the stories onto the pages of a notebook or photo album or store your mementos in a decorated and labeled shoe box.

Create a 1920s time capsule on disk, using a computer program like *The Amazing Writing Machine* (Broderbund) or *The Writing Center* (The Learning Company). Make some hard copies for your classroom library.

Create a giant collage. Cut the side from a large appliance box and paint it with gesso or tempera paint. Attach artifacts, articles, etc., to the dried surface with a glue gun.

Teacher's Note: Provide reference materials like *Ticket to the Twenties* by Mary Blocksma (Little, Brown and Company, 1993); *War, Peace, and All That Jazz* by Joy Hakim; *Fashions of a Decade: The 1920s* by Jacqueline Herald (Facts on File, 1991).

1920s Politics and Economics

On this page you will find a summary of some of the most significant political and economic events of the twenties decade. Further discussions of the topics can be found on the indicated pages.

Prohibition Called the "noble experiment," the Eighteenth Amendment, which made the manufacture, sale, and transportation of liquor illegal, became the law of the land on January 20, 1920. Read more about Prohibition and its consequences on page 32 of this book.

Women's Rights In August of 1920, women's long fight for the vote ended with ratification of the Nineteenth Amendment to the Constitution. For further information about women and the vote, see page 34 of this book.

The Red Scare Attorney General A. Mitchell Palmer, who hoped to be president, took advantage of the public's alarm over labor riots at home and Communist rebellions overseas. The result was a Red Scare that ruined many lives. Read page 16 for more information about the Red Scare.

Teapot Dome Scandal Warren G. Harding appointed friends to positions of power. They used their public offices for personal gain, accepting bribes from business interests and giving away priceless oil reserves. This scandal is one of the most blatant acts of government corruption ever seen. See page 17 for more details about the Teapot Dome Scandal.

Scopes Trial John Scopes was indicted for teaching the theory of evolution. The trial was intended to test the Tennessee law against teaching such theories and the First Amendment separation of church and state. For more details about the Scopes trial see page 40.

Immigration America's "open door" policy toward immigration ended with the institution of quota laws in 1921. Many Americans feared that they would lose their jobs to newcomers who were willing to work for less pay. Others were suspicious of newcomers with their different customs and languages. For more about immigration see page 39.

Stock Market Crash After the stock market fell on October 29, 1929, people lost their jobs, companies went out of business, and belt tightening became a way of life for everyone. A number of factors contributed to the fall of the stock market in 1929, including buying on margin and the ensuing selling panic. Read more about the stock market crash on page 28.

The Red Scare

Communism is a system of government in which most property and goods belong to the state. Its citizens are expected to share the proceeds, and there is a noticeable absence of classes. Anarchy is the absence of government authority or law, and its followers believe that all forms of government are oppressive and should be abolished. Both of these radical ideas were viewed as threats to America during the twenties.

In 1917, Russian communists revolted and took control of their government. Two years later, there were reports of similar revolutions throughout Europe. Some people feared that the communists wanted to take over the United States' government. When thousands of coal miners and steelworkers went out on strike in 1919, rumors led many Americans to conclude that such strikes were the result of communist infiltration.

In April, postal workers discovered bombs addressed to government leaders, including A. Mitchell Palmer, President Wilson's attorney general. Palmer, who wanted to become president, inflamed public opinion and began a campaign against the communists. Government agents invaded private homes, raided union offices, and deported 249 immigrants. Early in 1920, seven thousand people were arrested in an attempt to find the people responsible for sending the bombs. Palmer predicted a communist attack in May of 1920, but it did not materialize, and Palmer was discredited. In September of 1920, a bomb exploded on Wall Street, killing thirty-eight people and injuring a number of others, Although it apparently was an anarchist plot, Americans took it in stride.

The Sacco-Vanzetti Case

Nicola Sacco and Bartolomeo Vanzetti were anarchists and Italian immigrants who were arrested and tried for the holdup murder of a paymaster and his guard at a shoe factory in South Braintree, Massachusetts. Convicted in spite of strong evidence of their innocence, they were electrocuted. The debate over their guilt or innocence continues to this day.

Suggested Activities

Communism Have the students pool their pens and pencils in a central location, a large coffee can, for example. Whenever they need a pen or pencil they can take one from the container, but it cannot be one of their own. After experimenting with this system for a day or two, discuss with the class how they felt about sharing their utensils with others.

The Sacco-Vanzetti Trial Discuss the effects of public sentiment on criminal trials. Ask students if they believe the pair received a fair trial. Why or why not? Would the outcome be the same today?

Reference

The Sacco-Vanzetti Trial by Doreen Rappaport (HarperCollins, 1992).

The Teapot Dome Scandal

When the facts about the Teapot Dome Scandal emerged, the American people were shocked and outraged.

Who: President Harding appointed some of his friends to cabinet positions, delegating important responsibilities to men who were not qualified. Albert B. Fall was his Secretary of the Interior.

What: Congress designated land in California and Wyoming to ensure that enough oil would be available for the U.S. Navy in case of emergencies, i.e., war. Interior Secretary Fall secretly plotted to have these oil reserves turned over to his department. He then sold the drilling leases to private developers in return for bribes and kickbacks. A Senate investigation uncovered the scheme.

Where: This controversy centered on the oil reserves in Teapot Dome near Casper, Wyoming, and in Elk Hills, California.

When: Fall leased the oil reserves to oil companies in 1922. The scandal broke in October 23, 1923, two months after President Harding's death.

Why: Fall received over three hundred thousand dollars in cash, stock, and cattle in return for the lands. He was convicted for accepting a bribe and achieved the dubious distinction of becoming the first cabinet member in American history to go to jail.

Afterward: President Harding suffered a fatal heart attack before the Senate finished its report about the scandal. People were angry when they heard the news. It certainly changed their opinions of Harding. In Harding's defense, it is thought that he never personally profitted from these corrupt dealings.

Suggested Activities

Speculation Ask students how they think the public would have reacted if President Harding had been alive when the Senate completed its investigation of this scandal. Have them write a paragraph telling whether he should or should not have been impeached by Congress.

Corruption Interior Secretary Fall was the first cabinet member to serve jail time for his crimes, he was not the only crooked politician in Harding's administration. Assign groups to research other members of the "Poker Cabinet."

Crooks Harding may not have realized that the friends he appointed to office were ill qualified for their jobs or that some were crooks who would end up stealing money from the government. Brainstorm a list of ways a president can make sure that only qualified, honest people are given important government offices.

Presidential Knowledge

On the next four pages you will find some interesting facts about the four presidents who steered the U.S. through the Roaring Twenties. Select any or all of the following ideas and extensions for using these presidential profiles. Adapt them to suit your own classroom needs.

Additions Divide the students into four groups. Give each group a different profile. Assign them to do further research and add more facts to the pages.

Mapping Assign students to label a flag pin with the name of each president. Have them place each pin in the correct location of each president's birth on a large display map. Add to the map as you study presidents from other decades.

Vice Presidents On pages 19 to 22 no facts are given about the vice presidents except for their names. Have the students count off from one to four. Assign the ones to research Wilson's vice president, Thomas R. Marshall; the twos must research Harding's vice president, etc. Once the research is complete, let the groups meet and compare the facts that they found. Have them present their collective findings to the rest of the class.

First Ladies Divide the students into four groups, one for each first lady during this period. Write the names of the four first ladies on separate strips of paper and let each group draw a name. Tell them to find ten facts about their first lady, including her birthdate, place of birth, date of death, and education. Make a chart from a large sheet of white butcher paper and place it on a table or other flat surface. Ask the groups to write their facts and draw a portrait of their First Lady in the appropriate section of the chart. Display the completed chart on a classroom wall.

Descriptions With the class, brainstorm a list of words and phrases that aptly describe each president, for example, President Hoover—self-made millionaire, orphan, humanitarian, and insensitive. Ask the students to cite examples from his life story to explain each description.

Comparisons Pair the students to work on this project. Direct the pairs to fold a large sheet of drawing paper into fourths. At the the top of each fourth, write the name of a different president and then list each president's greatest achievements during his term of office. Ask the students to rate each president on a scale of one to five. One is lowest; five is highest. Have them write defenses for their choices on separate pieces of paper.

Campaign Buttons Have the students create a campaign button for each president. Cut buttons from construction paper or cardboard. Include an original slogan and/or a picture or drawing of the presidential candidate.

Requirements Review the requirements for candidates for the office of president of the United States (see page 23) and the electoral process. For more on these topics see Teacher Created Materials #582 *Thematic Unit—U.S. Constitution.*

Woodrow Wilson

28th President, 1913–1921

Vice President: Thomas R. Marshall

Born: December 29, 1856, in Stanton, Virginia

Died: February 3, 1924

Party: Democrat

Parents: Joseph Ruggles Wilson, Jessie Janet Woodrow

First Ladies: Ellen Louise Axson; Edith Bolling Galt

Children: Margaret, Jessie, Eleanor

Nickname: Professor

Education: Ph.D.

Woodrow Wilson

Famous Firsts: Wilson was the first president to hold a press conference. He was also the first president with a Ph.D. and the first president to travel to Europe.

Achievements:

- With the ratification of the Sixteenth Amendment, income tax became legal. The Federal Reserve Act was instituted; this agency controlled the money supply.

- In 1917 he was forced to declare war against Germany.

- On January 8, 1918, Wilson presented his Fourteen Points for Peace. He negotiated the Treaty of Versailles, which also established the League of Nations.

- For his work in ending World War I, Wilson was awarded the Nobel Peace Prize.

Interesting Facts:

- After suffering a stroke, Wilson allowed his wife to handle lesser government details. She decided which matters were important enough to bring to his attention.

- Wilson typed his own letters on a typewriter that could type in either English or Greek.

- Wilson did not have an inaugural ball because he considered them to be frivolous.

- Wilson's second wife, Edith, was a descendant of Pocahontas.

- The Wilsons kept a flock of sheep on the White House lawn to keep the grass trimmed. After the lambs' wool was sheared, it was sold, and the money was donated to the Red Cross.

Warren Gamaliel Harding

29th President, 1921–1923

Vice President: Calvin Coolidge

Born: November 2, 1865, in Corsica, Ohio

Died: August 2, 1923

Party: Republican

Parents: George Tyron Harding, Phoebe Elizabeth Dickerson

First Lady: Florence Kling De Wolfe

Children: None

Nickname: Wobbly Warren

Education: B.S. from Ohio Central College in Iberia, Ohio

Warren Gamaliel Harding

Famous Firsts: Harding was the first president to ride to his inauguration in an automobile and to speak over the radio. He was also the first president to be born after the Civil War. Harding was the first president since the Civil War to speak in the South on behalf of equal rights for African Americans.

Achievements:

- With his promise of a "return to normalcy," Harding won the 1920 presidential election by a landslide.
- A new government office called the Bureau of the Budget was proposed; its job was to make a formal, unified budget for government spending.
- He signed the Immigration Restriction Act of 1921, establishing the first quotas on immigration in the nation's history.
- From November 1921 to February 1922, Harding convened the Washington Conference for the Limitation of Armament. The U.S., Great Britain, Japan, France, and Italy all agreed to limit the size of their armies.

Interesting Facts:

- Despite the fact that he had voted for prohibition when he was a senator, Harding secretly stocked the White House with illegal bootleg liquor.
- Harding held numerous poker games which often ran late into the night. Many of his cabinet members were among the regular players. During one game, the president gambled away a complete set of White House china.
- Warren Harding was the first president for whom women could vote.
- Harding's Airedale, Laddie Boy, delivered the president's newspaper to him every day. Laddie Boy even had his own valet.

John Calvin Coolidge

30th President, 1923–1929

John Calvin Coolidge

Vice President: Charles G. Dawes

Born: July 4, 1872, in Plymouth, Vermont

Died: January 5, 1933

Party: Republican

Parents: John Calvin Coolidge, Victoria Josephine Moor

First Lady: Grace Anna Goodhue

Children: John; Calvin, Jr.

Nickname: Silent Cal

Education: Cum laude graduate of Amherst College; admitted to the bar in 1897

Famous Firsts: His first cabinet meeting lasted only 15 minutes.

Achievements:

- Coolidge often said "The chief business of America is business" and encouraged the speculative "Bull Market" of 1928. He also felt that the business of government was to keep out of business. In keeping with his policy, tax laws favorable to business were passed.

- Twice Coolidge vetoed the McNaury-Haugen farm bill, which provided that the government would purchase surplus crops from U.S. farmers at a fixed price and resell them abroad.

- Coolidge promoted commercial aviation, and in 1926 Congress passed the Air Commerce Act, which placed commercial aviation under federal regulation.

- In 1928 the Kellogg-Briand Pact was ratified. Countries who signed the agreement promised not to use war as a tool of national policy.

Interesting Facts:

- While Coolidge was governor of Massachusetts, the police force in Boston went on strike. He sent in the state troops and upheld the decision to fire the strikers. In a terse reply to the AFL leader, Samuel Gompers, Coolidge said, "There is no right to strike against the public safety by anybody, anywhere, any time."

- Coolidge was known for his thriftiness. In order to economize at the White House, guests were served plain ice water in paper cups.

- Nicknamed "Silent Cal" because he never wasted words, his reply to a woman who bet that she could get him to say at least three words was, "You lose."

Herbert Clark Hoover

31st President, 1929–1933

Herbert Hoover

Vice President: Charles Curtis

Born: August 10, 1874, in West Branch, Iowa

Died: October 20, 1964

Party: Republican

Parents: Jesse Clark Hoover, Hulda Randall Minthorn

First Lady: Lou Henry

Children: Herbert, Jr.; Allan

Nickname: Chief

Education: Degree in engineering from Stanford University

Famous Firsts: Hoover was the first president born west of the Mississippi River and the first to have an asteroid named after him. He was the first president to have a telephone on his desk.

Achievements:

- Hoover sponsored the Agricultural Marketing Act of 1929 to help farmers dispose of surplus crops.
- Because Hoover was blamed for the Great Depression and its effects on the American people, homeless camps were referred to as "Hoovervilles," and the newspapers that homeless people slept under were called "Hoover blankets."
- Hoover believed that business and labor should cooperate to end the financial crisis and did not believe in government aid for the unemployed and the homeless.
- Hoover hoped that the Smoot-Hawley Tariff of 1930, which raised tariff rates to record high levels, would increase sales of U.S. products by raising the price of imported goods.
- In 1932 Hoover created the Reconstruction Finance Corporation to loan billions of dollars to businesses and banks to help them out of the depression.

Interesting Facts:

- A self-made millionaire, Hoover managed the distribution of 18 million tons of food to starving people in Europe during World War I. The term "hooverize" was coined in honor of him; it meant to conserve food for the war effort.
- Herbert Hoover never accepted his salary for the presidency.
- Herbert Hoover held honorary degrees from over 50 American universities.
- Hoover and First Lady Lou Henry both spoke Chinese and often used the language to protect themselves from eavesdroppers.
- A 1962 survey conducted by the School of Engineering and Applied Science at Columbia University named Thomas Edison and Herbert Hoover the two greatest engineers in U.S. history.

Could You Be President?

Article II, Section I, of the Constitution establishes certain requirements for the presidency.

No Person except a natural born Citizen, or a Citizen of the United States, at the time of the Adoption of this Constitution, shall be eligible to the Office of the President; neither shall any person be eligible to that Office who shall not have attained the Age of thirty five Years, and been fourteen Years a Resident within the United States.

List the basic requirements for the office of the president of the United States:

1. _____

2. _____

3. _____

Based on this information, discuss and answer the following questions.

1. Do you think these are fair requirements for the office of president? Why or why not?

   _____

   _____

2. What additional requirements do you think should be added to this list? For example, should there be an educational requirement—college graduates only—or should anyone of any educational level be allowed to run?

   _____

   _____

   _____

3. What personal and social qualities should a person who is running for the presidency possess? Explain each of your choices.

   _____

   _____

4. In retrospect, which of the four presidents during the twenties did the best job while in office? What were the qualities that gave him this edge?

   _____

   _____

   _____

5. Would you want to be president? Why or why not? What do you think you could take to the presidency that is currently missing?

   _____

   _____

   _____

The President Game

Use this game to test students' knowledge of the four presidents on pages 19 to 22.

Preparations: Copy the quiz cards below and glue each to a separate 3" x 5" (7.5 cm x 12.5 cm) index card. Laminate and make additional quiz cards, if desired.

Playing Directions:

Divide the class into four teams; assign each one a different president. Direct the groups to make a sign with their president's name on it. Shuffle the cards and draw one to read aloud. The group whose president is described should raise their sign. Continue in this manner until all cards have been read. Keep score, if desired. **Note:** The correct presidents' names have been provided on each card for easy reference.

Quiz Cards	
return to normalcy *(Harding)*	blamed for the Great Depression *(Hoover)*
He did not accept his salary as president. *(Hoover)*	died suddenly while in office *(Harding)*
Silent Cal *(Coolidge)*	Teapot Dome Scandal occurred during his term *(Harding)*
the first president to travel to Europe *(Wilson)*	became a widower while in office *(Wilson)*
the first president to speak over the radio *(Harding)*	During his term income tax became law. *(Wilson)*
"The chief business of America is business." *(Coolidge)*	His vice president was Charles G. Dawes. *(Coolidge)*
His Vice president was Calvin Coolidge. *(Harding)*	the first president to have an asteroid named after him *(Hoover)*
was a Democrat *(Wilson)*	the first president with a Ph.D. *(Wilson)*
a graduate of Stanford; degree in engineering *(Hoover)*	promoted commercial aviation *(Coolidge)*
known for his thriftiness *(Coolidge)*	did not believe in government aid for the unemployed *(Hoover)*

Election Facts and Figures

	Election of 1920	Election of 1924	Election of 1928
Democrats	James M. Cox of Ohio ran for president with Franklin Roos as his running mate.	West Virginia lawyer John W. Davis was nominated on the 103rd ballot.	New York Governor Alfred E. Smith, was the first Roman Catholic nominated by a major political party.
Republicans	Senator Warren G. Harding of Ohio ran for president; his running mate was Governor Calvin Coolidge of Massachusetts.	Calvin Coolidge was unanimously nominated. Charles G. Davis was Coolidge's running mate.	Secretary of Commerce Herbert Hoover ran a low-key campaign, hinting at an early end to poverty.
Issues	Democrat Cox urged Americans to work hard for a lasting peace while the Republicans attacked Wilson's record, claiming he had been unprepared for war, and discredited Wilson's League of Nations.	Republicans feared voters might hold the scandals of the previous office against them, but Coolidge's direct manner following Harding's death seemed to steady the country.	While Smith was campaigning for religious tolerance, Republicans printed pamphlets claiming Smith would be the pope's servant if elected.
Slogans	Harding promised a "return to normalcy."	Keep cool with Coolidge.	Hoover coins said, "Good for 4 years of prosperity."
Results	Harding-Coolidge received 404 electoral votes to Cox-Roos 127.	Coolidge won with 382 electoral votes versus 136 for Davis. Robert M. LaFollette of the Progressive Party received 13 electoral votes.	Hoover carried 40 of the 48 states with a 444 to 87 electoral vote.

More About the Elections

Each of the three elections in the 1920s focused on different issues, and different campaign promises were made. Here are some ways to use the Election Facts and Figures on page 25. Use the activities and projects which best suit your classroom needs.

1. Make copies of page 25. Randomly assign one election to each pair of students. Instruct the pairs to complete any or all of the following activities:

   a. Find out more about the men nominated for president: where they were born, childhood and schooling, their political backgrounds, etc.

   b. Make a poster for each candidate's campaign. Include appropriate campaign promises and qualities that would make that person a good president.

2. The 1924 presidential campaign was the first national party convention broadcast on radio. Divide the students into small groups and have them write a short radio announcement introducing the presidential candidates. Let them perform their announcements for the whole class.

3. During the 1928 Coolidge-Smith race for the presidency, the Republicans claimed that Smith (a Roman Catholic), if elected, would be controlled by the pope in Rome. Coolidge was unaware of this campaign tactic, but many of the midwesterners who read such claims believed them.

   a. With the class discuss whether they think a religious leader would dictate a president's policies.

   b. Ask students how they think Coolidge might have reacted had he known about the claims his own party made against Smith.

   c. Write this question on the board and tell students to write a response: If Alfred E. Smith were to run for office today, would his religion be as big an issue as it was in 1928? Why or why not?

4. Read Article II of the Constitution to find out the procedures for electing the president. Follow the procedures to conduct a mock class election for president and vice president.

   a. Define electoral votes and explain how the number of electoral votes apportioned to each state is determined. Find out how many total electoral votes there were in each election.

   b. Make a flow chart to show how the electoral college works.

5. Use information about the various elections to construct graphs or charts. Let the students construct pie charts or graphs to show these results. For a prepared activity see Presidential Graphs and Charts on page 27.

Presidential Graphs and Charts

Think about the presidential elections in terms of math. It's easy if you follow the directions below. Write all answers on this page as directed.

Election of 1920

Warren Harding was the Republican candidate, and James M. Cox was the Democratic candidate in the 1920 election. A socialist, Eugene V. Debs, also ran, as did some independent candidates. Look at the popular vote figures for this election below. Make a pie chart of the percentages to show the results.

Candidate	Popular Vote	Percentage
Harding	16,143,407	60%
Cox	9,130,328	34%
Debs	919,799	4%
Others	534,534	2%

Election of 1924

Republican Calvin Coolidge ran against Democrat John W. Davis in 1924. Progressive Robert La Follette also ran. Read the electoral vote figures for all three candidates below. Create a graph to show the election results.

Candidate	Electoral Votes
Coolidge	382
Davis	136
La Follette	13

Coolidge				
Davis				
La Follette				

100 200 300 400

Election of 1928

The election of 1928 pitted Republican Herbert Hoover against Democrat Alfred E. Smith. A handful of others also ran. Use the electoral and popular vote figures to make pie graphs of the election result percentages.

Candidate	Electoral Vote	Popular Vote
Hoover	84%	58%
Smith	16%	41%
Others	0	1%

Electoral Vote

Popular Vote

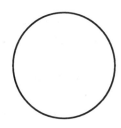

Teacher's Note: Statistics for this page were taken from the book *American Timeline: Entering the 20th Century, 1901–1939* by Tim McNeese (Milliken Publishing Co., 1986).

Black Tuesday

On Tuesday, October 29, 1929, the stock market collapsed. Ten billion dollars in stock were lost in very heavy trading in only a few hours that day. Stocks that had sold for twenty to forty dollars a share just a few weeks ago now sold for pennies. High rollers who had been speculating in the market were immediately bankrupted. President Hoover's claim that the country's business was "on a sound and prosperous basis" proved to be tragically incorrect. In the weeks and months that followed, the effects were even more profound. Five thousand banks failed and closed their doors, causing over nine million people to lose their savings accounts. For the first three years following the stock market crash, an average of 100,000 jobs were lost each week. Since so many people were out of work or in danger of losing their jobs, people began to economize and avoided unnecessary purchases. As demand for goods decreased, businesses were forced to lay off workers, adding to unemployment. Soon, people's money ran out, and they were unable to pay their mortgages and other debts. They lost their homes, cars, and other valuables. Hardship became a way of life. Some families were forced to live in shacks made of discarded lumber and cardboard. These shanty towns became known as "Hoovervilles," and the newspapers they used for blankets were called "Hoover blankets."

Suggested Activities

Cause and Effect Briefly review with the class the relationship between cause and effect. Establish that cause is the reason something happens and effect is the action that takes place in response to the cause. Discuss with the class some of the following causes and effects from the paragraphs about Black Tuesday.

a. People economized and avoided unnecessary purchases (cause); demand for goods decreased and businesses laid off additional workers (effects).

b. The stock market crashed (cause); high rollers were bankrupted, banks failed, and nine million people lost their savings (effects).

c. Millions of people were out of work (cause); they began to economize (effect).

Priorities Group the students and have them make a list of at least 15 ways they think families during the depression began to economize. In whole group compare the different lists. Extend the activity with a discussion of how they would economize today if their family support member suddenly lost his/her job. Compare these methods with the lists for depression families.

Simulated Crash To help students understand how and why the stock market crashed, engage them in a simulation activity. Complete directions and game cards can be found on pages 85 to 88 in Teacher Created Materials #480—*American History Simulations.*

Understanding the Stock Market

In order to fully comprehend the implications and importance of the stock market crash, it is necessary to understand how the stock market works. Use the background information on this page and the flow chart on page 30 to help students learn the terms and ways of the stock market world. Follow this lesson with the activities on page 31.

As a pre-test, write each term on the chalkboard or overhead projector. Ask the students to number a sheet of paper from one to ten. Read a definition aloud (see answer key) and have students write the correct answer, choosing from the list.

Make a copy of the What Is the Stock Market? section for each pair or small group. Instruct the pairs or groups to find definitions for each of the 10 words within the text of the story and compare the answers to their pre-test responses.

What Is the Stock Market?

The business of buying and selling stocks is known as the stock market. Stocks, or shares in a company, are bought and sold in a place called the stock exchange. The most important stock exchange is on Wall Street in New York City. Usually the stock market reflects the business world. If business is good, the value of stocks, or shares in a business, go up, and it is called a bull market. If business is poor, however, stocks go down, and the market is called a bear market.

During the twenties the prevailing market was a bull market. By 1927 more and more people were getting rich from their investments in the stock market. This led others to use all their savings to invest in the market for a handsome profit or dividend. After all, they wanted to cash in on an easy way to make money. Some people began buying on margin, which means they would pay a percentage of the purchase price and then borrow the rest of the money from the stockbroker who sold them the stocks. When a panic of wild selling caused the prices of stocks to plummet in mid-1929, a devastating crash followed. Stockbrokers had to sell as the stock prices fell, leaving people with worthless stock holdings. Worse yet, stockholders still owed money on their stocks because they had purchased them on margin. People had to sell their homes or cars to repay their loans. Businesses began losing money and were forced to lay off masses of workers. Banks that loaned the money in the first place had to close their doors when the loans went unpaid. Today the Securities and Exchange Commission, or the SEC, as it is commonly called, regulates the stocks and bonds, or securities, market. An independent government agency, the SEC was formed in 1934 with Joseph P. Kennedy as its first chairman.

1. bear market _____

2. stockbroker _____

3. dividend _____

4. stock exchange _____

5. SEC _____

6. bull market _____

7. panic _____

8. stock _____

9. margin _____

10. stock market _____

Stock Market Flow Chart

Make a transparency of this page for use on the overhead projector. Read and discuss the steps together.

To create a hands-on activity, make enough copies of this page for each group of students (cover up the numbers before copying). Cut apart the rectangles from one page and place them in an envelope labeled Stock Market Flow Chart. Continue in the same manner for all copies. Give each group an envelope and direct them to put the flow chart in correct sequence. To make this activity self-correcting, write a code on the back of each section. For example, step 1 could be labeled ab, step 2 cd, step 3 ef, etc.

1. The XYZ Games Company manufactures board games, and it wants to expand its operation. Since money is needed to buy a new plant and more sophisticated equipment, the company looks for people who will invest money in the company.

2. XYZ Games Company decides to go public and sells shares, called stocks, in its company. Ten thousand shares are offered at $100 each. Everyone who buys a share in the company becomes a part owner, or shareholder, of the XYZ Games Company.

3. The new games are a huge success and earn large profits for the company. Stockholders are given a percentage of the profits; this percentage is called a dividend.

4. XYZ continues to do well and demand for stock in the company increases. However, there are only 10,000 shares. People are willing to pay more than the $100 asking price for the shares. Soon, XYZ stock sells for $200 per share.

5. As more and more people try to enter the booming stock market, a new purchasing tactic becomes common—buying stocks on margin. That is, a small amount is paid down, and the rest of the money is borrowed from the stockbroker, the person who sells stocks. People are using their entire savings just trying to cash in on these windfall profits.

6. In October of 1929 a panic ensues when everyone begins to sell and no one wants to buy. What this means to the stockholder is that when the stock price drops, the stockbroker sells it. The stockholder not only loses his down payment, but he still owes the stockbroker the remaining purchase price borrowed to buy the stock. The stockbroker, in turn, owes money to the bank from which the money was borrowed.

7. In order to repay these loans, some people sell their houses and cars. No one has enough money to buy games from XYZ Company, so it closes its doors. Hundreds of workers lose their jobs. Banks close due to unpaid loans—they have no money.

8. A depression sweeps the country. Twenty-five percent of the work force is unemployed. All kinds of people, both rich and poor, are affected. Business activity declines, prices fall, and unemployment remains high for the next ten years.

Reading the Stock Pages

Have you ever looked at the stock quotations in your daily newspaper? At first glance, it may seem like a jumble of numbers. But there is an easy way to make sense of it all. A sample from a stock page is shown below. This entry is from the New York Stock Exchange. Following the entry is an explanation of all the letters and numbers.

Stock	Div.	PE	Sales	Close	Chg.
Albertsn	.52	18	3126	29 $^7/_8$	+ $^3/_8$
AmExp	.90	14	10170	39 $^5/_8$	+ $^1/_8$
BankAm	1.84	9	13144	54 $^1/_2$	- $^1/_4$

Stock Stock refers to the name of the company, usually abbreviated, i.e., Albertsn stands for Albertsons (a grocery chain); AmExp for American Express (credit card company); BankAm for Bank of America.

Div. Div. is the abbreviation for dividend. The dividend is expressed in dollars and cents. For Albertsons, the dividend is 52 cents; for American Express it is 90 cents; for Bank of America it is one dollar and 84 cents.

PE. The price-earnings ratio (PE) is the ratio of the current market price of a share of stock to the corporation's annual earnings per share. The PE of Alberstons is 18.

Sales This figure shows in thousands the number of shares sold that day. 3,126,000 shares of Albertsons were sold; 10,170,000 shares of American Express were sold; 13,144,000 shares of Bank of America were sold.

Close Close refers to the price of the last share sold. Albertsons closing price was $29 $^7/_8$; American Express' closing price was $39 $^5/_8$; Bank of America's closing price was $54 $^1/_2$.

Chg. Chg. is the abbreviation for change. This figure shows the difference between the closing price today and the closing price the day before. Note that the closing price for the day before is not shown on the chart. The plus (+) sign before the change means that the price is up; a minus sign (-) indicates the price is down. The change for Albertsons is up $^3/_8$ and American Express is up $^1/_8$. Bank of America is down $^1/_4$.

Note: Some stock pages contain more than one list of stocks. The New York Stock Exchange lists the top 1,500 stocks traded. The American Stock Exchange lists the top 750 stocks. NASDAQ contains the top 1,500 stocks traded.

Think and Discuss

With a partner solve the following problems based on the stock market sample at the top of this page. Check your answers with another pair.

1. Figure out the closing price of Albertsons for the day before.
2. What was Bank of America's closing price for the day before?
3. Which stock sold the most shares that day?
4. What is the difference between the number of shares sold in the two highest sellers?
5. What is the average amount of dividends paid by the three companies?
6. What is the difference between the two lowest closing prices?

Prohibition: An Overview

What Is Prohibition? Prohibition, or the outlawing of the consumption of all alcoholic beverages, may seem like an unmanageable task on a national level. At the beginning of the twentieth century, there were those who thought otherwise. At the outset, the majority of Americans supported the Eighteenth Amendment, believing that a world without liquor would be a better place. After a few years it became apparent that its drawbacks outweighed any possible benefits.

Alcohol Related Problems Alcoholism was a prevalent problem in nineteenth century America. Men would drink away whole paychecks, leaving no money to support their families. Some women's groups, religious groups, and reformers fought for prohibition. Many states became dry; that is, they passed laws which made it illegal to buy or sell liquor. The fight did not stop there, however, because some people wanted to make the whole nation dry. This would take a constitutional amendment.

Why Prohibition Was Supported Prohibition was supported by religious groups who believed that drinking was sinful. Business leaders also favored prohibition, thinking it would reduce absenteeism at work. Other groups blamed poverty, disease, and crime on alcoholism. Physicians spoke out about the dangers of alcohol consumption to unborn babies and noted that in large families where the parents drank, the children were often mentally retarded. When the United States entered World War I, a strong argument for personal sacrifice and the need for grain to aid in the war effort led Congress to pass the Eighteenth Amendment. It read: "After one year from the ratification of this article the manufacture, sale, or transportation of intoxicating liquors within, the importation thereof into, or the exportation thereof from the United States and all territory subject to the jurisdiction thereof for beverage purposes is hereby prohibited." Ratified by 36 states in January of 1919, the Prohibition Amendment took effect in January 1920.

Why Prohibition Did Not Work Prohibition made drinking more attractive to many people. Consumption of alcohol by women and young people increased. Gangsters like Al Capone of Chicago took over the illegal activity of selling liquor. Speakeasies popped up all over the country—by 1933 there were more than 200,000 speakeasies throughout the United States. Prohibition laws became the most disliked and disobeyed laws in U.S. history. Congress did not foresee problems with enforcement of the law and did not provide enough money for agents.

Effects of Prohibition The restrictions of Prohibition probably caused the outrageous behaviors of the 1920s. Speakeasies, nightclubs, and blind pigs had abundant business. Making "bathtub gin" and brewing beer became popular pastimes. Disregard for Prohibition created contempt for other laws and made crime a big business.

Reliving Prohibition

Help students understand the issues and implications of Prohibition with any of the following activities. Choose those that are best suited to your classroom situation and modify the assignments as needed.

Class Debate Have two groups of students prepare for and debate this question: Could the lessons of Prohibition be applied to the current drug problem in the United States?

Response Ask students to respond in writing to this question: Should Prohibition be reinstated? Why or why not? Discuss their written responses in whole group.

Deja Vu Discuss the following questions with the class: What if Prohibition were reinstated in the U.S. today? How would it be enforced? What measures would have to be taken to ensure that organized crime does not profit from the measure?

New Age Prohibition Divide the students into small groups. Their assignment is to determine something that should be prohibited at school, like chewing gum, soft drinks, etc. Have them write a law outlawing the sale or consumption of the product. Let the students draw up appropriate punishments for use of the product and outline ways that the law will be enforced. Have the groups share their projects with the rest of the class. As an extension, take one of the prohibitions schoolwide. See if any of the other classes jump on the bandwagon.

Campaign Many communities and large corporations have created campaign slogans, signs, and materials against drinking and driving. Assign individuals or pairs to create a poster that might help convince people not to drink and drive. Display all the posters on the classroom walls.

Words Write the words temperance and prohibition on the board. Ask students to explain the difference between the two words. Have the students define these and other Prohibition-era terms: dry, bootleggers, rumrunners, speakeasies, temperance, teetotaler, jake leg, blind pig.

Cause and Effect Pair the students. Direct them to write a list of five cause and effect statements related to Prohibition. For example: Because Prohibition outlawed drinking, some people who had never drunk before decided to drink alcoholic beverages. In whole group, identify the causes and the effects of all the statements.

Lessons Learned Americans learned that some kinds of prohibition must be done by persuasion and education (from *War, Peace, and All That Jazz* by Joyce Hakim).

1. Ask the students if they agreee or disagree with this statement. Have them give reasons for their responses.

2. In small groups, let the students list some other lessons learned from the era of Prohibition.

To Read For more information about Prohibition, read the October 1993 issue of *Cobblestone,* which focuses on the era. Pages 44 and 45 contain an annotated bibliography of related books. To order a back issue call 1-800-821-0115.

The Nineteenth Amendment

The framers of the Constitution of the United States gave little, if any, thought to the rights of women. Women could not own property in most states, and very few worked outside the home. Education for women was considered unnecessary and frivolous. As essential as women were to the family structure, they did not have equal status with men on any front.

For years women lobbied for their right to vote. Susan B. Anthony was a major force in organizing women in the mid-nineteenth century. Her fight for the right to vote was carried on by the suffragists in the early 1900s. Marches and motorcades were staged; banners were displayed with the women's pleas. Police arrested and jailed some of these women, but that did not deter them.

Finally, in June of 1919, Congress passed the Nineteenth Amendment. The necessary states quickly ratified the amendment, and it became law on August 26, 1920. With just 28 words, women were granted full rights to vote.

Suggested Activities

Response Have students respond in writing to the following questions. Why was the Nineteenth Amendment necessary in the first place? Did the Constitution imply that women could vote? Did it ever state in the Constitution that women could not vote?

Banners Pair or group the students. Have them create posters or banners, complete with slogans for the suffragists to use, and stage a mock demonstration. Role play with male students giving the female students reasons why women should not be able to vote; females can respond appropriately.

Note: Design posters or banners, using a computer program like *Print Shop Deluxe* (Broderbund, 800-521-6263) or *Super Print* (Scholastic, 800-541-5513). Tape the printed panels together and glue them to sheets of tagboard for more durability. Attach cardboard strip handles to posters for individuals. Let groups of students help carry the long banners.

Research Give students a choice of these three suffragists to research: Elizabeth Cady Stanton, Susan B. Anthony, or Carrie Chapman Catt. Make a group chart divided into three sections, each headed with the name of a different suffragist. Let students write at least one interesting fact in the appropriate section.

Writing Assign students to write one page about the Nineteenth Amendment, using either of the following titles: What the Nineteenth Amendment Means to Me or How the Nineteenth Amendment Changed the Course of History.

References

For a prepared teaching unit on women's suffrage, write to National Women's History Project, 7738 Bell Rd., Windsor, CA 95492 or call (707) 838-6000 for more information.

You Want Women to Vote, Lizzie Stanton? by Jean Fritz (G. P. Putnam's Sons, 1995).

The Fight for Birth Control

Teacher's Note: *The information on this page may not be suitable for all students. Please review it carefully before presenting it to your class.*

As a child Margaret Sanger witnessed her own mother's struggle with numerous pregnancies. In thirty years the woman conceived eighteen times and gave birth to only eleven living children. Weakened and exhausted by the many pregnancies, Sanger's mother died at the age of fifty. This living example inspired Sanger to pursue her mission in life—to deliver information about birth control to all women.

Margaret Sanger

In the year 1910, very little in the way of contraception was available. The Comstock law, which declared it obscene to provide information about birth control, had been passed. Poor, uneducated women had nowhere to turn. It was, indeed, a frightening situation. As a public-health nurse in New York's lower east side in 1912, Sanger was appalled by the conditions endured by the women she saw. Poverty, disease, and death rates were high; yet, the women continued to bear children. Determined to provide relief for these women, Sanger wrote a series of articles about reproduction for a socialist newspaper. When one was declared obscene under the Comstock law, Sanger fought back and founded a newspaper called *Woman Rebel*. Before she could be tried for her crime, Sanger left for Europe, where she studied what other countries were doing about family planning.

On her return to the U.S., the case was dismissed, but Sanger was not through. In 1916 in Brooklyn, New York, she and her sister, Ethel Byrne, opened America's first birth control clinic. Arrested for keeping a public nuisance, the pair was jailed for thirty days. The resulting publicity served to help Sanger's cause, and New York state revised its laws.

In the meantime, Sanger's personal life was disintegrating. Her five-year-old daughter died of pneumonia, and Sanger and her husband divorced. Later, she married a wealthy businessman who wholeheartedly supported her efforts. Through it all she continued her fight for birth control and in 1921 organized the American Birth Control League, now known as Planned Parenthood. Six years later she helped plan the first world population conference which was held in Geneva, Switzerland.

In 1966, six years after the first birth control pills for women were marketed, Margaret Sanger died. Thanks to the efforts of this indomitable woman, information about effective birth control is now widely available.

Suggested Activity

Discussion With the class discuss this question: How did Margaret Sanger contribute to the quality of life for women in the early part of the twentieth century?

Uncovering the KKK

There are those who maintain that certain races, religions, and nationalities are superior to others. The Ku Klux Klan, commonly called the KKK, is one such group. To learn more about their activities, particularly in the 1920s, read the information below.

What It Is The Ku Klux Klan is an organization of people who hate other groups of people, particularly those who are not native born, Protestant, and white. Members of the KKK especially oppose the advancement of Blacks, Jews, and other minorities.

Origins In 1865 or 1866 a group of Confederate Army veterans in Pulaski, Tennessee, formed a social club. The name Ku Klux Klan is taken from the Greek word *kyklos* which means circle and the English word *clan*. Members of this group believed in the superiority of whites and began terrorizing African Americans to prevent them from voting. Klan members wore robes and white hoods to hide their identities and even draped sheets over their horses. They burned crosses to frighten Black, Jews, and other minorities and threatened, beat, and lynched their victims. The Ku Klux Klan spread rapidly throughout the southern United States. Following a Congressional investigation in 1871, the Klan activities diminished.

A Return After World War I, agricultural depression, migration, and other social and economic factors caused social unrest. The Klan philosophy was broadened to include anti-foreign, anti-Catholic, anti-Semitic and anti-urban principles. At its height in the mid-twenties, the revived KKK had between 4 ¹/₂ and 6 million members and heavily influenced the government of at least seven states. Some called it "The Invisible Empire."

Election of 1928 During the 1928 presidential election, the group played a pivotal role. Al Smith, the Democratic presidential candidate, was an Irish Catholic. The KKK maintained that if Smith were elected, the Catholic pope would rule America from Rome. Many believed their propaganda, and Smith was easily defeated.

Suggested Activities

Terms Write the words *hate, bigotry,* and *racism* on the chalkboard. With the class define and discuss what they mean. Discuss why people hate and what role fear plays in discrimination.

Threats In 1924 African American actor Paul Robeson was threatened by the KKK for playing the role of a black man married to a white woman in *All God's Children Got Wings.* Discuss with the students the acceptance of mixed-race couples today. What are the concerns about these relationships? How does society view such relationships?

Quote One Grand Wizard, a KKK leader, once said, "Negroes, Catholics, and Jews are the undesirable elements in America." Ask students to respond to that statement.

The Harlem Renaissance

Terms *Harlem* is an area of New York City which became a black community during the twenties. *Renaissance* means a rebirth or revival of intellectual and/or artistic achievement. Michaelangelo was a product of the Italian Renaissance, which marked the transition from medieval to modern times.

Purposes This literary movement gave black men and women a chance to create their own images and express their unique experiences as Black Americans in the United States. College-educated African American men and women flocked to Harlem to share their ideas, write poetry and novels, paint pictures, and produce movies. Their written and artistic works celebrated the vitality of life and reflected the black cultural heritage.

Harlem became a great center of African American culture as the community found a new sense of independence and developed pride in its own traditions.

Problems The rapid growth of the area brought its own set of problems, including overcrowding and high rents. The death rate for African Americans was almost twice that for whites. Unable to support themselves with their art, African Americans often took menial jobs. White people flocked to Harlem, which they thought of as an alien and exotic place, for the fresh nightlife, but they regarded Blacks as primitive and one-dimensional. Blacks were not accepted as equals and could not be served in many of the Harlem theaters and clubs where they performed. Writers and artists alike worked hard to dispel these myths, and the resulting art and culture are testimonies to their diverse abilities.

Suggested Activities

Poets Read some selections from the poetry of both Langston Hughes and Countee Cullen. Who employed a more traditional style? Which style do the students prefer? Why?

Musicians Duke Ellington and Louis Armstrong played jazz music. What instrument did each play? How did they get a start in their careers? How were their styles alike and different?

Novelist Zora Neale Hurston used her skills as an anthropologist to explore the culture of her Florida hometown. She listened to and collected folk tales such as "Why the Porpoise Has His Tail on Crossways" and "How the Woodpecker Nearly Drowned the Whole World." Have students choose one of these titles and write a creative tale.

Discussion Have students discuss how African Americans' experience of life in the twenties differed from that of their white counterparts.

Back to Africa During the early twenties Marcus Garvey, who owned a fleet of steamships, urged African Americans to be proud of their African roots and suggested that they return to Africa to establish a free black nation. With the class discuss whether the Back to Africa movement would have helped or hurt the African American's position in America had it been carried out.

The Amazing Schomburg Collection

The Schomburg Center for Research in Black Culture, named for Arthur A. Schomburg, contains the largest collection of material about the history, writings, and art of the African American community. All the items can be looked at or copied by anyone, but must remain in the library and cannot be checked out. The story of how this collection came into existence is an interesting one.

Arthur A. Schomburg

Arthur A. Schomburg was born in San Juan, Puerto Rico, on January 24, 1874. Little is known about his early life. As a young adult, Schomburg participated in an interracial history club. He noted with some interest that the whites were knowlegeable about their history, while the black participants were not as familiar with their heritage. It was this experience that prompted Schomburg to learn all he could about the history of Blacks. He started with the contributions of Blacks to the history and culture of Puerto Rico.

In 1891, Schomburg moved to New York City. He supported himself by teaching Spanish and traveled, lectured, and wrote. He began working for the Banker's Trust Company on Wall Street in 1923. His steady salary allowed him to continue collecting. His collection of relevant documents, books, plays, letters, sermons, music, and artwork grew, and by 1926 Schomberg had collected over 11,000 books and items for his purpose. The Carnegie Corporation paid Schomburg $10,000 for his collection, a handsome sum in those days, and this collection was made part of the New York Public Library system at the 135th St. Library. When Schomburg retired from Banker's Trust in 1929, he became the curator of the Division of Negro Literature, History, and Prints, a position he held until his death in June of 1938.

An invaluable resource for students and writers during the Harlem Renaissance, the collection now contains manuscripts from Countee Cullen and Langston Hughes, prominent figures of the Harlem Renaissance. For his efforts in putting all this information together, Schomburg received the William E. Harmon Award for outstanding work in the field of education.

Suggested Activities

Act It Out Prepare and present a short skit about the Schomburg Center. An excellent prepared text can be found in the book *Take a Walk in Their Shoes* by Glennette Tilley Turner (Puffin Books, 1989).

Discussion Discuss the importance of Schomburg's collection and its impact on the culture of the African American.

Coming to America

Immigration was not new to the 1920s, but the complexion for the situation changed dramatically in the early part of the twentieth century. From its earliest years the United States of America had an open door policy toward immigrants, placing few restrictions on the number of people entering this country. It was not until 1882 that the first law was passed banning people from a specific country. The Chinese Exclusion Act forbade Chinese laborers because it was feared that they would work for lower pay. In 1907 a "gentleman's agreement" between the United States and Japan barred Japanese immigrants.

In the early 1900s there were two groups who sought to have the doors closed to certain ethnic members. American laborers feared that they would lose their jobs to new immigrants, who were willing to work for lower wages. A second group believed that the newcomers were inferior. Still, it was not until 1917 that restrictions were in place, preventing thirty-three different categories of people from obtaining entry to the U.S.

Immigration in the 1920s changed in another important way. Prior to 1880 newcomers originated mostly from countries in northern and western Europe. When the immigrant population shifted to southern and eastern European countries, some Americans became alarmed at the customs and languages. World War I placed a temporary halt to the problem as very few people came to America during that period. Once the war ended, the wave of immigrants rose steadily, with over 600,000 people arriving in 1921. With the passage of a new law that same year, immigration was limited by a quota system. The National Origins Act of 1924 established severe quotas for southern and eastern European countries. For example, 100,000 Italians had arrived in one year in the early 1900s, but the new quota limited Italy to 5,082 people per year; Greece was allowed only 307 people per year, while Russia was permitted 2,784 per year. Not until the 1960s, when Lyndon Johnson became president, did those quota laws change.

Suggested Activities

Respond Have the students respond to this question: Are quota laws for immigration fair or necessary? With the class, discuss some possible solutions for this dilemma.

Charts Divide the students into groups and have them make charts comparing 1920s immigration with current immigration. Include topics such as length of travel, mode of travel, cities of entry, and countries of origin.

References

Do People Grow on Family Trees? by Ira Wolfman (Workman Publishing, 1991)
Teacher Created Materials #234 *Thematic Unit—Immigration.*

The Monkey Trial

The Scopes Trial, sometimes called the Monkey Trial, was the best-known trial of the decade. Its main issue was the public school's right to teach the science of evolution.

Background Information: Evolution is the science which traces life on earth through millions of years of development from simple one-celled creatures through increasingly complex plants and animals to humans. Fundamentalist Christians, among others, believe in the creation story that is told in the Bible. The Bible states that the world was created in six days. In 1925 the Tennessee legislature passed a law prohibiting the teaching of any theory that denies the creation story of the Bible. It also prohibited teaching that man evolved from lower animals.

When and Where: The trial took place in Dayton, Tennessee, in the summer of 1925.

How the Trial Came About: In 1920 the ACLU (American Civil Liberties Union) offered to pay the legal expenses of anyone interested in testing the Tennessee law. The ACLU believed that the law was unconstitutional since the First Amendment provides for the separation of church and state. This amendment guarantees that the government cannot pick your beliefs, force you to attend church, or make you pay taxes to support a particular church, for example.

The Players: The defendant is John Scopes, a 24-year-old school teacher.

Clarence Darrow, an attorney and an agnostic (someone who is unsure whether there is a God or not), represents Scopes.

William Jennings Bryan heads up the prosecution for the state of Tennessee. Well known and well liked, Bryan has run for president three times and is a fundamentalist.

Arguments: Darrow attempted to prove that church doctrine is being imposed on public schools because the 1925 Tennessee state law tells citizens what they should believe. Bryan accused Darrow of wanting to slur the Bible.

Settlement: Scopes was convicted and fined $100 but this conviction was later reversed because of a small legal error.

Present Day In the 1980s, Arkansas and Louisiana passed laws requiring public schools that teach evolution to devote equal time to the teaching of creationism. In 1987 the Supreme Court found that these laws are in conflict with the First Amendment.

Suggested Activities

Opinion Ask the students their opinions about the following question: Would the outcome of the case be the same if it were tried today? Why or why not?

First Amendment. Assign the students to find and copy the text of the First Amendment. With the class discuss what it means.

Public Opinion Most people at the time did not take the trial seriously and called it the Monkey Trial. What part do monkeys play in the trial?

The Walt Disney Story

Although his own childhood was not happy, Walt Disney brought joy to children worldwide with his cartoon characters and theme parks. His best known creation is Mickey Mouse, described by Disney as "a nice fellow who never does anybody any harm." Walter Elias Disney debuted on December 5, 1901, the fourth of five children born to Elias and Flora Disney. Disney's early years were spent on a farm in Marceline, Missouri, where he developed an interest in drawing. The family moved to Kansas City in 1910. Disney continued his art and at 14 enrolled in classes at the Kansas City Art Institute. World War I provided the opportunity to leave his abusive father. He quit school after ninth grade and, too young for combat, served as a Red Cross ambulance driver in France. In 1919, Disney and a friend formed an art company and made some animated cartoons.

Walt Disney

Four years later he moved to California, where he and his brother, Roy, began Walt Disney Productions. Disney created a character he called Mortimer the Mouse. His wife, Lillian, suggested a name that was less stuffy, and Mickey was born. In 1928, with Disney providing his voice, Mickey Mouse starred in *Steamboat Willie,* the first cartoon to use *synchronized* sound (sound that matched the movements and actions in the film).

The success of Mickey Mouse was only the beginning. In the thirties Mickey acquired a number of cartoon pals, including Donald Duck, Pluto, Minnie Mouse, and Goofy. Disney continued to explore and innovate, developing better technologies to tell his stories. The thirties brought the world's first feature-length animated film, *Snow White and the Seven Dwarfs,* and in 1941 animation and live action were combined for the first time in *The Reluctant Dragon.* In the 1950s, Disney added live action features, nature films, and feature films for television. His cast of characters was featured on weekly television programs and on the daily *Mickey Mouse Club.* Disney earned more than 30 Academy Awards for his work.

Walt Disney died in 1966, but the studio he founded continues the Disney tradition, bringing new technology to films. Disney's spirit lives on in his memorable characters and theme parks.

Suggested Activities

Mickey Designs Mickey Mouse has been merchandised in numerous forms: on clothing, eating utensils, jewelry, etc. Group the students and have them design a new product featuring Mickey Mouse.

Flip Book See page 42 for directions to make animated flip books.

Catalog Brainstorm a list of Disney films. Categorize them by technique (live, animated, etc.) or by subject "lands," like fantasy land, tomorrow land, etc.

Reference

The Man Behind the Magic by Katherine and Richard Greene (Viking, 1990).

A Flip Book

Although he was not the first to produce animated films, Walt Disney pioneered modern techniques that have set the standard for excellence in the industry. One method that animators use to track their character's movement is to draw figures in a flip book. Make your own flip book, following the directions below.

Materials: scissors, typing or copy paper, stapler, pencil, fine-point black marker

Directions:

1. Cut several pieces of paper in 3" x 5" (7.5 cm x 12.5 cm) rectangles. Stack the paper, keeping the edges of the paper even. Staple the pages together at one end.

2. Plan how you want your character to move. On a separate sheet of paper, sketch your character's movements in different positions.

3. When you are satisified with your sketches, begin with the last page of your book. With pencil, sketch your character's first position near the outside edge of the page.

4. Skip two or three pages and sketch the character's second position on this page. Continue skippng pages and sketching other positions until you have drawn the last position.

5. Go back and fill in the empty pages with the character's positions in sequence.

6. When the sketching is complete, flip the pages from the back to the front page. Note any movements that do not look right and fix them. Trace over your finished sketches with a fine-point black marker. Share your flip book with a partner.

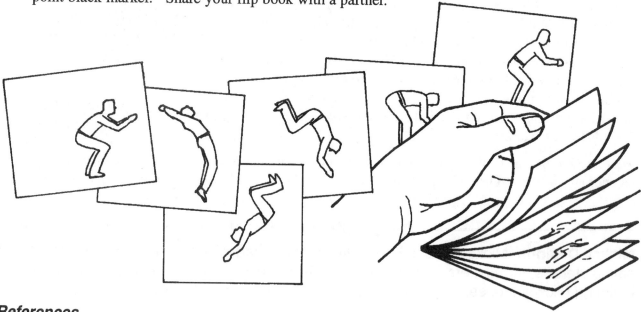

References

Make Your Own Animated Movies and Videotapes by Yvonne Andersen (Little, Brown and Company, 1991). This text also contains information about using the *Video Works* program on your Macintosh computer to produce cartoons.

Cartooning for Kids by Marge Lightfoot (Firefly Books, 1993).

Animated Films by Rhoda Nottridge (Crestwood House, 1992).

The Master Clown of Silent Movies

Charlie Chaplin

He was an actor, director, and a music composer. A man of extremes, his life went from utter poverty to wealth, from being adored to being hated to being honored around the world. His name was Charlie Chaplin, the best and most-loved pantomime artist who ever lived. Chaplin was born Charles Spencer Chaplin in London on April 16, 1889, to Charles Chaplin, Sr. and Hannah, popular music hall entertainers. At the age of five, Chaplin made his debut, and his singing and dancing delighted the audience. When he was 17, Chaplin and his brother Sydney found work with England's most popular pantomime artist. Chaplin learned quickly to use his body instead of words to create laughter. Four years later, Chaplin and the troupe were off to America.

Although the show was not a particular success, Chaplin was, and he landed a contract with the movies. At first, Chaplin was uneasy with the acting style of the day, which consisted mostly of exaggerated facial gestures and body movements coupled with a lot of slapstick. Sound was not recorded, and there were no scripts. Sets were close to one another and noisy; in a word, the scene was chaotic. Chaplin determined to make the best of the situation and transformed himself with baggy old pants, a tight jacket and tie, a derby, huge shoes, and a skinny bamboo cane. The Little Tramp was born. Audiences loved him, and after only three years he was a world-famous star and a millionaire.

During the depression of the thirties, the tide turned against him. Some people accused Chaplin of being un-American because he had never become a U.S. citizen. Others called him a communist and claimed he had not paid taxes. Amid this and other criticisms, Chaplin left for Europe in 1952. He settled in Switzerland with his fourth wife and children. Not until April 1972, when he was to receive a special Academy Award for his lifetime achievement, did he return to the U.S. New audiences had discovered his work, and he was once again the beloved master clown of the movies.

Suggested Activities

Pantomimes In the movie *The Gold Rush*, Chaplin eats his boot and makes it appear that he is enjoying a special treat. Let students take turns pantomiming this scene or another from any of his films.

Charades Write the names of some of Chaplin's films on separate index cards. Ask for volunteers to pantomomine the titles for the rest of the class: *The Kid, The Gold Rush, City Lights, The Tramp, Modern Times.*

Skits Group the students and have them write and act skits with no words. Let the groups take turns performing for the rest of the class.

Satchel Paige and the Negro League

During the 1920s, organized baseball was separated into all-white and all-black leagues. Players on teams in the Negro leagues, as they were called, received low wages, and equipment was shabby. Because many businesses would not accommodate African Americans, the players sometimes had to sleep on the bus or in the dugout at the ball park. Despite these hardships, the players remained dedicated to their work.

Leroy "Satchel" Paige, regarded as one of the greatest pitchers in the history of baseball, started his career in the Negro leagues.

Leroy Robert Paige was born to John and Lula Paige of Mobile, Alabama, in 1906. His nickname, Satchel, originated either from his satchel-sized feet or from

Satchel Paige

the baggage (satchels) that he carried on his job at Union Station. From playing sandlot baseball, Satchel Paige progressed to teams in the All-Negro Southern Association. While playing for the Mobile Tigers in 1924, he was paid according to how collections went among the spectators. If enough money had been collected, he received $1 for the game. If not, he was given a keg of lemonade. From this humble beginning, Paige went on to command one of the highest salaries in baseball in his day. Often booked as a solo star, he guaranteed nine strikeouts in three innings to any team that agreed to his asking price ($500 to $2,000 per game).

Professional baseball leagues became integrated in 1947, and African American players were accepted as members of major league teams. The following year, Paige was hired by the Cleveland Indians. He was the oldest "rookie" ever and the first African American pitcher in the American League. When Paige retired from the St. Louis Browns five years later, he had been named most valuable pitcher. Satchel Paige was inducted into the National Baseball Hall of Fame in 1971.

Suggested Activities

Discussion Discuss with students: How many professional baseball players today do they think would still play the game if their pay depended on how much was collected from the spectators?

Math Problems During his lifetime Satchel Paige played about 2,500 games and won 2,000 of them. What percentage did he lose? Share some other statistics about Paige and let students write their own word problems. For example, of 2,500 games, 300 were shutouts and 55 were no-hitters. In 1933 Paige pitched 31 games and lost only 4.

Others Some other Negro League players include Josh Gibson, Cool Papa Bell, Oscar Charleston, and Judy Johnson. Challenge students to find out more about these players.

References

Take a Walk in Their Shoes by Glennette Tilley Turner (Puffin Books, 1989).

Satchel Paige by David Shirley (Chelsea House, 1993).

The Story of Negro League Baseball by William Brashler (Ticknor & Fields, 1994).

The Sultan of Swat

Babe Ruth

George Herman Ruth was one of the most famous baseball players of all time. A flamboyant figure, he brought excitement to an otherwise tranquil sport. A southpaw in a game where most of the players were right-handed, and with a barrel-shaped body and spindly legs, he did not fit the image of a world-class athlete.

Born in 1895, Ruth grew up on the streets of Baltimore, fending for himself, and by the age of eight had gotten into trouble. Young George was sent to a Catholic boys' home, where he played baseball. An invaluable team member, he could play just about any position.

In 1914 Ruth began his career with the Baltimore Orioles, at that time a minor league team. Later that year, Ruth joined the Boston Red Sox. There, he served as a pitcher while also showing his prowess as a hitter. Because he could hit the ball harder and farther than any other team member, he held two positions—in some games he pitched and in other games he played in the outfield. By 1918, Babe Ruth was recognized as the best left-handed pitcher in baseball. He also led the American League in home runs. Boston's owner, in need of money, sold Ruth to the New York Yankees after the 1919 season. As a Yankee, Ruth concentrated solely on hitting and playing the outfield, and immediately, he shattered a number of records and brought baseball to a new level.

Formerly, baseball had been a pitcher's game, but Ruth changed all that; now it was a hitter's game. Ruth set many records that stood unchanged for years. In 1920 he broke the 1884 record of 24 home runs in one season by hitting 54. The next year he hit 59 homers and scored a total of 177 runs. In 1927 Ruth hit 60 home runs, a record that stood for 34 years. Attendance at games increased so much that the Yankees built Yankee Stadium, sometimes known as "the house that Ruth built." At forty, fat from eating and drinking too much, Ruth hit three home runs in his last professional baseball game. It was an amazing feat by an amazing athlete.

Suggested Activities

Records Ruth's 1927 record of 60 home runs stood unbroken until 1961. Have students research to find the following information: What player broke Ruth's record? Who currently holds the home run record? What is this record?

Candy Bars People mistakenly think that Baby Ruth candy bars were named after Babe Ruth. Assign students to research the true story behind the name of the candy bar.

Salary In 1930 Babe Ruth signed a contract for an unprecedented $80,000 per year, more money than the president of the U.S. earned. Compare Ruth's salary to today's presidential salary and to baseball players' earnings.

Another Babe Babe Didrikson Zaharias was another famous athlete of this period. An outstanding golfer, softball star, tennis player, swimmer, and diver, this Babe won Olympic medals in three track and field events in 1932. Compare her achievements with those of some contemporary female athletes.

Transatlantic Flight

Charles Lindbergh

After World War I, the availability of surplus equipment and trained pilots led to the growth of commercial aviation. Barnstormers presented air shows and provided short rides for the public, and airplanes carried mail across the country. Soon attention focused on the possibility of transatlantic flight. In 1919 a wealthy hotel man offered a $25,000 prize to anyone who could fly nonstop from New York to Paris.

Such a flight was extremely hazardous. The pilot would have to fly thousands of miles over a stormy ocean and would face rain clouds, dense fog, and even icebergs. Over the next eight years several pilots, including explorer Richard Evelyn Byrd, tried and failed. Then, in May of 1927, an unknown airmail pilot named Charles Lindbergh accepted the challenge.

His plane, the *Spirit of St. Louis*, was ill equipped for such a dangerous undertaking. It had no radio, and the pilot's seat was a wicker chair. Because the plane carried as much fuel as possible, there was no room left for any excess weight. All that Lindbergh carried on board with him was a quart of water, a paper sack full of sandwiches, a map, letters of introduction, and a rubber raft. Staying awake and alert throughout the 33 ½ hour flight proved to be a major challenge for Lindbergh.

A raucous, cheering crowd greeted Lindbergh when he landed in Paris. After meeting European kings and princes, Lindbergh and the *Spirit of St. Louis* returned home, where he was showered with parades and celebrations. A world hero at the age of 25, Lindbergh's feat inspired a popular song, a dance, and popular fashions.

Lindbergh refused numerous offers for moneymaking opportunities following his historic flight. He continued to be a strong advocate of aviation and flew 50 combat missions in World War II. In 1953 he earned a Pulitzer Prize for *The Spirit of St. Louis*, which chronicled his historic flight.

Suggested Activities

Aviation History Teach students about the history of flight. Read aloud the book *The Wright Brothers: How They Invented the Airplane* by Russell Freedman (Holiday House, 1991). Discuss the adversities Lindbergh faced.

Female Pilot In 1922 Bessie Coleman became the first licensed African American pilot in America. Because of the existing prejudice against Blacks, Coleman had to travel to France, where she learned how to fly. Coleman was honored in 1995 by the U.S. Post Office with a 32-cent stamp. Have students research this woman's background and accomplishments.

Earhart Amelia Earhart became as famous as Lindbergh when she flew solo across the Atlantic in 1932. In 1937 she attempted to fly around the world. Her plane disappeared somewhere in the South Pacific six weeks into the journey. Assign students to research what happened to Earhart and her co-pilot.

Mapping Assign students to create a map of Lindbergh's flight across the Atlantic.

References

Lindbergh by Chris L. Demarest (Crown Publishers, Inc., 1993).

Barnstormers & Daredevils by K. C. Tessendorf (Macmillan, 1988).

A Space Pioneer

Robert Goddard's dreams of space and interplanetary travel were influenced by two books—*The War of the Worlds* by H. G. Wells and *From the Earth to the Moon* by Jules Verne. After reading and rereading both novels, he was convinced that space travel was indeed a possibility. A Massachusetts physicist, Goddard first conducted research on improving solid fuel rockets.

In 1923, Goddard began testing a rocket with liquid fuel, gasoline, and liquid oxygen, and three years later he launched the world's first successful liquid-fueled rocket. It flew 184 feet (56 m), reached an altitude of 41 feet (12.5 m), and traveled at 60 miles (100 k) per hour.

From 1930 to 1935 Robert Goddard continued to launch rockets, attaining higher and higher speeds and heights. He developed ways to guide rockets and even devised parachutes which allowed the rockets to return safely to earth. Sadly, the U.S. government took little note of these accomplishments during Goddard's lifetime. Not until 24 years after his death in 1945 would the dream of landing on the moon become a reality.

Suggested Activities

Bottle Rockets Make outdoor bottle rocket launchers. For each rocket you will need 1 brightly colored ribbon bow, 1 thumbtack, 1 1-quart (1 L) soda bottle with a cork to fit, ½ cup (120 mL) of vinegar, 1/2 cup (120 mL) of water, 1 teaspoon (5 mL) of baking soda, and a 4" (10 cm) square piece of paper towel. With the thumbtack attach the bow to the cork. Pour the water and vinegar into the bottle. Place the teaspoon of baking soda in the center of the paper towel square, roll it up, and twist the ends. Go outside and drop the paper towel packet into the bottle. Fit the cork tightly into the mouth of the bottle and set it on a flat surface. Stand back and watch the cork fly into the air.

The Isaac Newton Connection Newton's three laws of motion explain how rockets work and why they can fly in outer space. Read about the life of Newton. See pages 95 and 96 in Teacher Created Materials #493 *Focus on Scientists* for hands-on experiments.

Discussion With the class discuss the importance of Goddard's work and how his early experiments paved the way for space exploration. Ask students for their opinions about why the U.S. government did not pay much attention to his work at that time.

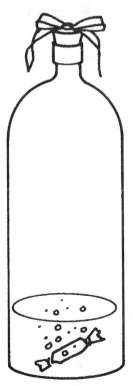

References

Robert H. Goddard by Karin Clafford Farley (Silver Burdett Press, 1991).

The War of the Worlds by H. G. Wells. (Various editions)

From the Earth to the Moon by Jules Verne. (Various editions)

Star Light, Star Bright

Annie Jump Cannon was an extraordinary woman, particularly for her time. In the late 1800s, very few women progressed in their educations beyond grade school or high school. Few careers were open to women, and it was expected that they marry and raise families. Cannon was born on December 18, 1863. Her father was a shipbuilder, and her mother was a typical homemaker except for an interesting hobby—stargazing. When Cannon was very young, she and her mother would climb to the rooftop of their home and spend hours observing the stars through a telescope. As a schoolgirl, Cannon excelled in her studies, and her teachers convinced her parents to provide her with a higher education.

Annie Jump Cannon

At 16 Cannon began studies at Wellsley College. After graduation, she worked in the Harvard Observatory where she assisted in cataloging stars. Star pictures were taken by combining photographs with telescopes that were specially equipped with prisms. The resulting photograph showed the different bands of light produced by each star. Using the information from the photographic plates, Cannon classified the stars.

Astronomers had been using an A, B, C classification system, but Cannon found a better arrangement that is standard for astronomers even today. Between 1915 and 1924 Cannon produced nine volumes of the *Henry Draper Catalog,* a guidebook for astrophysicists. This achievement made her famous. During her lifetime Cannon cataloged over 350,000 stars and also discovered five *novae* (stars that suddenly become brighter and then fade). In recognition of her pioneering work, Annie Jump Cannon was the first woman awarded an honorary doctorate from Oxford.

Suggested Activities

Hobbies Cannon's mother's hobby was stargazing, and she included Cannon in this fascinating activity. Discuss with the class how they think this early experience with the stars influenced Cannon's future work. Ask them about any hobbies they may have and how they became interested in those particular areas.

Numbering Through the course of her career Annie Jump Cannon catalogued over 350,000 stars. As a class project, draw 350,000 stars. Attach a large sheet of butcher paper to a classroom wall. When students have spare time (or use a rotating schedule), they can add stars to the sheet. Let students draw the stars or use a star-shaped stamp.

Prisms When she was a child, Cannon spent many hours enjoying the dancing rainbows produced by the prisms from her mother's candelabra. Hang some prisms in front of a classroom window and observe the light displays. For some information on making your own prisms see Teacher Created Materials #493 *Focus on Scientists.*

Homework Assign the class to observe the stars each evening for a week. In class each morning discuss their observations and any pictures they have drawn of the star formations they have seen.

Coming of Age

Margaret Mead

Margaret Mead was part of a revolution that changed the roles of men and women in society. In her work she sought to show people the need to live full, rich lives, unrestricted by society's limitations of male/female roles. Her goals were to bring about world peace, to promote multicultural understanding, and to help children everywhere.

Mead's story began on December 16, 1901, when she was the first born into a busy and unconventional household in Philadelphia, Pennsylvania. Both her mother, Emily Fogg, and her paternal grandmother, Martha Mead, had careers of their own at a time when it was highly unusual for women to work outside the home. As a sociologist Emily often spoke out about the living conditions of poor women. Martha Mead was an educator and school principal who directed her granddaughter's education. Because her parents' jobs required frequent moves, Mead had lived in 60 different homes by the time she was in junior high school. For Mead the moves were an adventure, and she adapted easily to each new environment. Of special interest to her was what made families so alike and yet so different.

After her 1923 graduation from Barnard College, she received a grant to do field work among the Polynesian people of Samoa. By her own admission, Mead knew little about what she was getting into or how to proceed, but she eventually developed a system for recording her experiences. Based on observations of 68 Manu'a village girls over a six-month period, she concluded that Samoan female adolescents experienced an easier transition to adulthood than did their American counterparts. The information Mead had so meticulously documented formed the basis of her dissertation at Columbia University and was published as *Coming of Age in Samoa: A Psychological Study of Primitive Youth for Western Civilization* (William Morrow, 1928). On later field studies in New Guinea and Bali, Mead employed the techniques of note-taking, interviewing, observing, and photographing that continue to be used by cultural anthropologists.

Margaret Mead did not slow down until 1978, when a serious illness caught up with her. On November 15, 1978, she died from pancreatic cancer. Nine national memorial services were held in memory of this great pioneering anthropologist.

Suggested Activities

Modern Anthropologists Ask students to imagine that they have received a grant to study the culture on a new planet. Direct them to make a booklet of notes, interviews, observations, and pictures of the adolescent boys and girls that they observe there.

Alike Yet Different Mead was curious about how families were alike yet different. Pair the students and have them take turns interviewing one another to find out how their families are alike yet different. Discuss the results with the whole group.

References

The Importance of Margaret Mead by Rafael Tilton (Lucent Books, 1994).

TCM #493 Focus on Scientists.

Revolutionizing the Auto Industry

Some people mistakenly think that Henry Ford invented the automobile. His name is synonymous with the auto industry because he improved the manufacturing process, making an existing invention affordable. In doing so, he changed American life.

Ford was born on July 30, 1863, on a farm near Dearborn, Michigan. From his childhood he showed an interest in engines, and at the age of sixteen he became a machinist. In 1888 he married Clara Bryant, who actively encouraged Ford to build and experiment with engines. By 1896 he had built his first automobile.

Seven years later Ford organized the Ford Motor Company. Because they were built individually by hand, cars were very expensive, and only a few Americans could afford them. Ford revolutionized the automobile industry by using an assembly-line method of production. This system of mass production saved money, and Ford

Henry Ford

was able to sell cars for less. In 1908 the Model T, sometimes known as the "tin Lizzie," debuted. The initial price was $850. In addition to the assembly-line technique, the Ford Company produced its own parts, glass, and steel. By eliminating the independent suppliers' high prices, the company saved even more money. These savings were passed on to the consumer, and Model T prices dropped to $290 in 1924. Between 1908 and 1927, over half the cars sold in the nation were Fords. Finally, automobiles were affordable for most families.

Ford also implemented some other changes in the work force. He reduced the work day from the standard nine hours to eight hours and increased the minimum wage to $5 per day. A profit-sharing plan for employees was instituted. With all of these incentives, workers flocked to the Ford plant. Despite these innovations, Ford products declined in popularity during the latter part of the twenties as General Motors began offering a wider variety of luxuries, such as different colors for exteriors, heaters, and yearly designs. In 1919 Henry Ford stepped down as president of his own company and named his son Edsel to take his place. Henry Ford died on April 7, 1947.

Suggested Activities

Imagine Affordable automobiles revolutionized living in the twenties. With the whole group, discuss the impact the car has made on present-day living. Ask students how life today might be different without cars.

Assembly Line Let individual students take turns putting together a snap-together model or a puzzle; have them record their time. Then group the students and direct them to assemble the model or puzzle by assigning each member a specific task. Have them compare their individual time with the group time of assembling the project. Ask them what they can conclude about assembly-line production.

Langston Hughes, an Everyday Poet

African American Langston Hughes is widely regarded as one of America's greatest poets. From the time he was in grade school he knew that he wanted to be a writer. Despite the adversities of a broken home and racial prejudice, Hughes was able to overcome these obstacles to fulfill his dreams.

Langston Hughes was born on February 1, 1902, in Joplin, Missouri, to Carrie and James Hughes. James Hughes had been studying law, but at that time in Missouri, African Americans were not allowed to become lawyers. Disillusioned, he moved to Toluca, Mexico.

Langston Hughes

Mrs. Hughes refused to go. She worked to support herself and Hughes. It was not always easy, but somehow they managed to get by. One important thing Carrie Hughes did was to pass on her love of reading to her son. By the time he had completed grammar school, Hughes had written his first poem, one in honor of his graduation.

Because his mother could not afford to pay for his college education, Hughes worked at various jobs, including deckhand, laundry worker, and dishwasher. One summer, he even earned money by working on his father's ranch in Mexico. During the long train ride there, Hughes composed a poem, "The Negro Speaks of Rivers," and sent it to a New York City magazine. James Hughes agreed to pay for his son's education, but only on the condition that he study engineering. When his son's poem was published later that summer, the elder Hughes relented. Hughes' long and successful career was off to a great start.

Altogether, Langston Hughes amassed a body of work that included poetry, plays, short stories, articles, and a series of books based on the character Simple. In addition, he founded theater companies throughout the United States for young people to learn playwriting and performing skills. Langston Hughes died on May 22, 1967.

Suggested Activities

Unpublished Poetry A children's book editor at Oxford University Press discovered Langston Hughes' unpublished manuscript, *The Sweet and Sour Animal Book* (Oxford University Press, 1994). Share these alphabet poems with the class. Direct the students to write some of their own alphabet poems in the style of Langston Hughes.

Biography Read aloud selections from a biography of Langston Hughes. Ask students to explain why Hughes deserves the title Poet Laureate of Harlem.

References

Extraordinary Black Americans: From Colonial to Contemporary Times by Susan Altman (Children's Press, 1989).

Instructor January/February 1995 ("Put on a Play About Langston Hughes" by Helen H. Moore, pages 66–70; "Kids' Art Brings Poems to Life" by Wendy Murray, pages 74–76).

Lives of the Writers by Kathleen Krull (Harcourt Brace & Co., 1994)

Essence of the Twenties

F. Scott Fitzgerald coined the phrase "The Jazz Age," and his short stories and novels captured the essence of the Roaring Twenties. His work reflected the indulgences and excesses of the times, as well as his personal struggles.

F. Scott Fitzgerald

Fitzgerald was born September 24, 1896, in St. Paul, Minnesota, to Mary and Edward Fitzgerald and named for a distant relative, Francis Scott Key. Because of Edward Fitzgerald's sporadic employment, the family was forced to move frequently. In order to cope, young Scott invented an inner world of his own. He read passionately and told imaginative tales. His mother encouraged him to excel and made no attempts to discipline him.

School bored young Fitzgerald. While his teachers lectured, he busied himself writing stories in the back of his geography or Latin book. His family sent him east to a small Catholic boarding school. There he quickly became one of the most unpopular students. He talked so much that he was considered a show-off, and he irritated his fellow students by endlessly analyzing them.

Although he failed the entrance exams for Princeton, he convinced the appeals committee that he would, indeed, make a good Princeton student and was admitted in 1913. In 1917 Fitzgerald left Princeton without a degree and joined the army.

While he was stationed in Alabama in 1918, he met Zelda Sayre, and the two married after the publication of his first novel, *This Side of Paradise,* in 1920. Like the characters in his second novel, *The Beautiful and the Damned,* the Fitzgeralds led lives of partying, drinking, and endless talking. *The Great Gatsby,* written in Paris and published in 1925, is considered by most readers to be Fitzgerald's best book.

Fitzgerald's drinking led to alcoholism, and Zelda suffered from mental illness. Their life together became increasingly unhappy. With the stock market crash of 1929, Fitzgerald's lucrative career came to an end. In the mid-thirties he left for Hollywood to work as a scriptwriter. At the time of his death in 1941 he was working on a novel, *The Last Tycoon.* Although it was unfinished, the manuscript was published as a series of unrevised chapters and notes.

Suggested Activity

Another Title *This Side of Paradise* was originally named *The Romantic Egotist.* Find out about other popular books that were written with other original titles in mind. For example, author Peter Benchley toyed with such titles as *Leviathan Rising* and *Great White* before he and his editor settled for *Jaws.* Read more fascinating stories behind book titles in *Now All We Need Is a Title: Famous Book Titles and How They Got That Way* by Andre Bernard (W. W. Norton & Company, 1994).

52

The Mount Rushmore Story

Gutzon Borglum

On March 25, 1867, John Gutzon de la Mothe Borglum was born in the Idaho Territory. His parents had immigrated to the U.S. from Denmark in 1864 and then traveled to the Territory by wagon train. Borglum's childhood was filled with Danish legends, the art of the old masters, and the culture of the Crow and Sioux. At 17 Borglum decided to devote his life to art.

Borglum studied under the famous French sculptor Auguste Rodin. His career flourished, and he received numerous commissions, both in the United States and Europe. Doane Robinson, secretary of the South Dakota Historical Society, asked Borglum to carve a sculpture in the Black Hills as a tourist attraction. A fanatic patriot, Borglum had no trouble saying "yes" to the plan. The site was Mount Rushmore, which rises 6,040 feet (1,804 m) above sea level. Towering 500 feet (152 m) above its nearest neighboring mountains, its granite face is approximately 1,000 feet (304 m) long and 400 feet (122 m) high. Borglum selected four presidents: George Washington to represent America's independence and the Constitution, Thomas Jefferson for his concern for westward expansion, Abraham Lincoln for his ability to hold the country together during the Civil War, and Theodore Roosevelt for his strong ties to South Dakota. Construction on Mount Rushmore did not began until late 1927. In 1929 Congress authorized it as a national memorial.

Borglum died before the completion of the monument in 1941, and his son Lincoln took on the remainder of the project. Today, the memorial grounds boast a visitor's center, an amphitheater, walks and trails, night lighting, and a museum of what was once Borglum's studio. The National Park Service regularly inspects and makes necessary repairs to the sculpture.

Suggested Activities

Controversy Direct students to research the concerns of Native Americans who inhabit the area. Find out about their own Crazy Horse memorial not far from Mount Rushmore.

Geology The Black Hills are one of the oldest geological formations on earth. Over the years a number of rock types built up over one another to form them. Mountains in the center of the hills are composed of igneous granite and metamorphic mica schist with fingers of granite squeezed in between the mica. Have students research igneous, metamorphic, and sedimentary rocks and create a chart which shows their characteristics and how they are formed.

Reference

The Mount Rushmore Story by Judith St. George (G. P. Putnam's Sons, 1985).

Jacob Lawrence and the Great Migration Series

Jacob Lawrence

One of the biggest population shifts in the history of the United States occurred during the period around World War I as hundreds of African Americans left their homes and farms in the South and migrated north to industrial cities in search of employment. Jacob Lawrence grew up knowing people on the move. Indeed, his own family was part of the first big wave of migration between 1916 and 1919. His parents met while they were en route to New York. His mother was from Virginia, while his father was born in South Carolina.

Lawrence was born in 1917 in Atlantic City, New Jersey. When he was 13, the family moved to Harlem in New York City. There Lawrence went to school and attended an after-school arts-and-crafts program. It was during this period that he decided to become an artist. At first, he just made designs but later progressed to painting street scenes. Inspiration was not far away. Friends and teachers helped him understand how his own experiences fit into the history of all African Americans in the United States. He also spent countless hours at the Schomburg Library (for more information about this library, see page 38), reading books about the great migration.

In 1940, at the age of 22, he began his Migration series. One year later it was completed. The series consisted of 60 numbered panels that told the story of the people who made the choice to move away from their homes. In his own words, ". . . I wanted to show what made the people get on those northbound trains. I also wanted to show what it cost to ride them." Each panel measured a mere 18" x 12" (45 cm x 30 cm), but altogether they made a powerful and moving statement.

Suggested Activities

Response Ask students to respond to this question: What sacrifices did people make in migrating North? If students have a hard time answering this, start by asking them what sacrifices they would have to make if they were to move to a different geographical location.

Creative Writing Direct the students to write a creative story about the family members who got left behind. Before beginning writing, brainstorm with the class and come up with some reasons that families or family members may have been left.

Art Series Create a class mural to chronicle an event at school. After the class has determined an event and planned panels that tell the story, divide the students into groups. Let each group work on a separate 18" x 12" (45 cm x 30 cm) panel. Display the finished panels on a classroom wall. Have the groups take turns telling the story.

Comparisons Compare the art of Jacob Lawrence with that of Romare Bearden, another artist who captured African American life in the 1920s.

Reference
The Great Migration by Jacob Lawrence (HarperCollins Publishers, 1993).

Empress of the Blues

Bessie Smith

One of the first great blues performers in the United States was African American Bessie Smith. Born in Chattanooga, Tennessee, in 1894, Smith lived the blues. Her family was poor, and to earn money she began singing on street corners when she was just a little girl. Smith made her professional debut at the age of nine at the Ivory Theater in her hometown. Later, she began traveling the southern circuit of segregated black theaters and tent shows. Sometimes they would perform special shows for white audiences. Everyone who heard Bessie Smith sing was mesmerized by her voice. After landing a recording contract with Columbia Records, her first release, "Down-Hearted Blues," sold over one million copies. Her many subsequent hits helped save the company from bankruptcy. At the peak of her career, she earned $2,000 per week, but, as was customary in those days with African American performers, she received no royalties. Altogether, Smith recorded 160 songs, many of which she wrote herself. Her trademark costumes—satin gown, headdress, and a long strand of pearls—earned her the title Empress of the Blues. A problem with alcohol coupled with the Depression led to the decline of Bessie Smith's meteoric career. In 1937 she was killed in a car accident and buried in an unmarked grave. Her family was unable to afford a headstone. In 1970 singer Janis Joplin and some other musicians decided to pay tribute to this long-forgotten talent. They purchased a headstone and had it engraved with the following epitaph: "The greatest blues singer in the world will never stop singing."

Suggested Activities

An Epitaph Discuss the meaning of the epitaph on Bessie Smith's headstone. Direct the students to design and draw an appropriate headstone for Bessie Smith's grave. Compose a new epitaph for the headstone.

Influence Bessie Smith's singing style influenced many later stars, including Mahalia Jackson, Billie Holiday, and Janis Joplin. Assign students to research these three singers, when they lived and how they sang. If possible, listen to some of their musical recordings.

Sing the Blues Divide the students into small groups. Have them write and perform a blues song that Smith might have sung.

References

Herstory: Women Who Changed the World edited by Ruth Ashby and Deborah Gore Ohrn (Viking, 1995).

Black American History Makers by George L. Lee (Ballantine Books, 1989).

From Ballots to Breadlines: American Women 1920–1940 by Sarah Jane Deutsch (Oxford University Press, 1994).

Kids Make Music by Avery Hart and Paul Mantell (Williamson Publishing, 1993).

Music Is My Language

Louis Armstrong

He grew up to be one of the greatest and best-loved jazz musicians the world has ever known. It was an amazing accomplishment, considering his youth. Louis Armstrong was born in the New Orleans ghetto on August 4, 1901. His family lived in a wooden shanty that had no electricity or plumbing. Nearby streets were lined with honky-tonks where drinks were cheap and fights were frequent. When he was just an infant, his father abandoned the family, and Armstrong was raised by his paternal grandmother. He attended school until the fifth grade, when he had to leave to help earn money by peddling newspapers and delivering coal.

An incident that occurred when he was 13 changed the course of his life. Trying to show off to a group of friends, Armstrong fired a pistol belonging to his stepfather. The prank sent him to the Colored Waifs' Home, a reform school for African American boys. As luck would have it, the school had a marching band, and Armstrong learned to play the cornet. After his release he went back to his former day jobs and spent nights combing the honky-tonks for a chance to sit in with the bands.

In 1922 Joe Oliver, the king of jazz trumpeters, asked Armstrong to join his band. It was during this time that Armstrong met and married Lillian Hardin, the band's young piano player. With her encouragement, Armstrong was eventually able to strike out on his own. By the mid-twenties he had organized the Hot Five, the Hot Seven, and the Savoy Ballroom Five. Throughout his career Louis Armstrong performed in Europe, South America, the Far East, Canada, and all over the United States. Music was his language, and he had no trouble communicating wherever he went. He is best-known for the new style that he created, giving his horn a voice-like quality, and for his distinctive singing voice. Nicknamed "Satchmo," a shortened form of satchel mouth due to his wide smile, Louis Armstrong died in 1971.

Suggested Activities

Collage Armstrong was also an artist. He enjoyed making collages and often carried scissors so he could cut out magazine and newspaper articles. After arranging them on a scrapbook page, he would tape his cutouts together. Assign students to collect movie ticket stubs, schoolwork, candy wrappers, and other items for one week. Have students arrange the items on a cardboard background and glue them to the surface to make a biographical collage which documents a week in their lives. (This idea was taken from the October 1994 issue of *Cobblestone:* "Louis Armstrong and the Art of Jazz.")

Definition. Jazz, a mix of ragtime, blues, and black spirituals, was invented by African Americans in the twenties. Listen to one or more recordings of Louis Armstrong's music, like *Louis Armstrong: The Hot Fives Volume I,* or Ella Fitzgerald and Louis Armstrong: *Ella and Louis.* Have the students draw abstract pictures using lines, marks, and shapes, while they listen to this music.

A Rhapsody in Blue

Although his life span was brief, George Gershwin achieved fame in his own time. Today he continues to be regarded as one of the great musicians of the twentieth century. A popular composer, he was the first musician to take jazz music into concert halls. His *Rhapsody in Blue* remains as a testament to his ability to combine a distinctive jazzy feeling with the sounds and techniques of classical pianists.

George Gershwin

Gershwin was born in Brooklyn, New York, in 1898 to poor Jewish immigrants. By the time he was twelve years old, Gershwin could play the piano. A few years later he dropped out of high school to work for a music publisher as a song plugger. Gershwin promoted songs by playing them for interested performers. In 1917 he became a rehearsal pianist for a musical play, and by the next year he had a steady job working for a music company. The company paid him $35 a week; that included all rights to publish any songs he wrote.

Gershwin's first hit song was "Swanee," sung by Al Jolson in 1920. One year later Gershwin wrote the score for a Broadway musical. Three years later he teamed up with his brother, Ira, to write the hit *Lady, Be Good!* which starred Fred Astaire on Broadway. Gershwin composed the music while Ira provided the lyrics for such popular songs as "I Got Rhythm" and "Embraceable You." By the beginning of the thirties, Gershwin had also written scores for films, including *Damsel in Distress* and *Goldwyn Follies*.

Gershwin also wanted to compose serious music, and in 1924, *Rhapsody in Blue* debuted, followed by *An American in Paris* in 1928. In 1929 he made his debut as a conductor for the New York Philharmonic Orchestra. In spite of his busy career composing for stage and films, Gershwin was able to make time to tour American cities and perform with major orchestras. Perhaps his most ambitious undertaking was the full-length opera *Porgy and Bess*. Based on a novel by DuBose Heyward, the story tells about the life of rural Blacks living in South Carolina.

Unfortunately, Gershwin's life ended all too soon; he died of a brain tumor at the age of 38, while at the height of his creativity. He left a legacy of beautiful and moving music. Generation after generation has rediscovered this national treasure, ensuring that Gershwin's music will never die.

Suggested Activities

Concerto Explain that *Rhapsody in Blue* is a concerto, a composition written for an orchestra and one or more instruments. If possible, listen to a recording of *Rhapsody in Blue.* Have the students identify the leading instrument. Listen to some concertos by some classical composers and compare them to Gershwin's concerto.

Contributions Discuss with the class Gershwin's contributions to the jazz movement. Compare how his jazz differed from that of Louis Armstrong or Duke Ellington.

1920s Inventors and Inventions

Among the items introduced in the 1920s were Kleenex®, Scotch® tape, the electric pop-up toaster, Eskimo Pies®, Wrigley's chewing gum, Band-Aids®, the Model A Ford, zippers, moving pictures with synchronized sound, Baby Ruth® candy bars, Rice Krispies®, and Popsicles®. The stories of their invention are as diverse as the products themselves. Here are three of them, along with some activities to get your students motivated to invent something of their own.

Kleenex

During World War I the Kimberly-Clark Company's newly developed cellucotton material was used to replace scarce cotton bandages. After the war, the company looked for new ways to market their product. Originally introduced as a disposable cloth for the removal of cold cream and facial makeup, its 65-cent price tag proved too costly for the average wage earner. When a later campaign emphasized, "Don't put a cold in your pocket," many people threw away their handkerchiefs forever and reached for a disposable Kleenex. Since then, Kleenex has become the best-selling facial tissue in the world.

Activity Divide the students into small groups and give each group a box of Kleenex. Ask them to list as many new uses for Kleenex as they can. Put a time limit on this project. Share all responses in the whole group.

Eskimo Pie

When a young boy could not decide whether to buy a chocolate candy bar or an ice cream sandwich, his dilemma inspired shop owner Christian K. Nelson to build a new frozen treat. In his spare time, he experimented with ways to get melted chocolate to stick to the outside of a slice of ice cream. One day a candy salesman provided him with some important information. By varying the amount of a key ingredient, cocoa butter, the chocolate stayed on the ice cream. Months later the I-Scream-Bar, later called the Eskimo Pie, was created.

Activity Have students bring ice cream, nuts, cookies, and syrups to school. Let them experiment with different ingredients to create a new frozen treat. As a group, have them choose a name for their favorite one.

Zippers

In the late 1800s even stylish clothes were fastened with laces, cords, or rows of buttons. Getting dressed or undressed could take up to half an hour! Whitcomb L. Judson, a prolific inventor, invented a new way to fasten his shoes. His first slide fastener was cumbersome, but continued efforts produced a practical, smooth-working zipper. First used by the U.S. Navy for flying suits, the zipper was popularized when B. F. Goodrich used it in a new line of rubber boots.

Activity Have the students make a list of all their clothes that have zippers. Tell them to imagine that all their zippers have been replaced with buttons. How would that affect their time getting dressed? Discuss whether they prefer buttons or zippers on their clothing.

References

Teacher Created Materials #232 *Thematic Unit: Inventions.*

Teacher Created Materials #496 *Focus on Inventors.*

Steven Caney's Invention Book by Steven Caney (Workman Publishing, 1985).

Twentieth-Century Inventors by Nathan Aaseng (Facts on File, 1991).

The Real McCoy: African-American Inventions and Innovation, 1619–1930 by Portia P. James (Smithsonian Institution, 1989).

Inventors' Quiz

On this page you will find a list of some 1920s inventions followed by the first names of their inventors. Uncover their last names by solving the problems in the box below. Every time you find that answer under the spaces in the clues, write the corresponding letter on the line. When you are through, you will know all of the inventors' last names.

A 595–495 = _____   B 285÷3 = _____   C 360÷4 = _____   D 364–279 = _____

E 195÷3 = _____   F 280÷4 = _____   G 150–75 = _____   I 240÷3 = _____

J 180÷3 = _____   K 131–76 = _____   L 250÷5 = _____   M 270÷6 = _____

N 240÷6 = _____   O 105÷3 = _____   R 180÷6 = _____   S 91–66 = _____

T 300÷60 = _____   U 99–89 = _____   W 60÷4 = _____   Y 135–115 = _____

1. frozen foods, Clarence   __95__ __80__ __30__ __85__ __25__ __65__ __20__ __65__

2. automatic traffic signal, Garrett   __45__ __35__ __30__ __75__ __100__ __40__

3. liquid-fueled rocket, Robert   __75__ __35__ __85__ __85__ __100__ __30__ __85__

4. Band-Aids, Earl   __85__ __80__ __90__ __55__ __25__ __35__ __40__

5. zipper, Whitcomb L.   __60__ __10__ __85__ __25__ __35__ __40__

6. Scotch tape, Richard G.   __85__ __30__ __65__ __15__

7. Eskimo Pies, Christian K.   __40__ __65__ __50__ __25__ __35__ __40__

8. Model A, Henry   __70__ __35__ __30__ __85__

9. colored motion pictures, George   __65__ __100__ __25__ __5__ __45__ __100__ __40__

10. synchronized sound/animation, Walt   __85__ __80__ __25__ __40__ __65__ __20__

Everyday Dress in the 1920s

The 1920s brought revolution in styles of dress, especially for women and children. Read about the changes for each group and then do one or more of the activities.

Children Traditionally, children were dressed as miniature adults. In the twenties, one-piece rompers for infants and playsuits for older boys and girls were introduced.

Teenagers Fashion had overlooked the teen years, taking young people straight from childhood to adulthood. When teens went to fight in World War I, a new market developed, and fashions just for teenagers were created. Magazines like *Seventeen* emerged for this new teenage market.

Women Hemlines rose for the first time in history and exposed women's legs. The thick, cotton stockings available at the time were quickly replaced with rayon. Head-hugging cloche hats fit over the short, bobbed haircuts sported by most women. Flesh-colored, all-in-one undergarments replaced restrictive, tight-laced corsets and camisoles. Women plucked their eyebrows and wore rouge and lipstick.

Men Styles became more relaxed and lighter, thanks to the sporting influence. Tennis sweaters and polo shirts were allowed for casual, as well as sporting, attire. Lindbergh's transatlantic flight spawned a cult following and a new look: leather jackets and helmets worn with goggles. Raccoon coats were popular.

Suggested Activities

- Actress Clara Bow epitomized the 1920s look. With her cupid-bow lips and kohl-rimmed eyes she became known as the "It Girl". Find a picture of Clara Bow (an excellent resource is *Fashions of a Decade: The 1920s* by Jacqueline Herald). Compare her look with today's fashionable look. Have students search through magazines to find their idea of today's "It Girl"; make a class collage of all the pictures.

- Swimwear was quite modest in the 1920s. Bathing suits were less restrictive but still required short-sleeved or sleeveless tunics over thigh-covering bottoms. In women's tennis, the knee-length tennis dress was introduced, but it had to be worn with white stockings. Designer Rene Lacoste introduced his soft collared, short-sleeved polo shirt with an alligator motif (still seen today) for men. Coco Chanel designed golfing outfits of jersey which made movement much easier and more comfortable. Ask students to find other 1920s influences that are still around today. Have students draw some sports fashions from the 1920s.

- Bobs were worn by over 90% of the American women during the twenties. Read F. Scott Fitzgerald's short story "Bernice Bobs Her Hair." Assign the students to write their own stories about a traumatic haircutting experience.

- Electric sewing machines were first introduced in the twenties. Discuss what impact this invention had on the fashion world.

- Let students design fashions; see page 61 for a prepared activity.

A 1920s Fashion Designer

Here is your chance to become a famous designer of the 1920s. Draw and design the clothing as directed in each section below.

1. Cloche hats hugged the head to fit over the short bobs that women wore. Draw a cloche on the head below. Add appropriate makeup, such as rouge, lipstick, and kohl for eyeshadow. 	2. Tutmania was the rage in 1922 after King Tut's tomb was discovered. Draw and design a bracelet and necklace with an Egyptian theme.
3. Lindbergh popularized the leather jacket after his transatlantic flight. Design a leather jacket for men in the twenties.	4. Swimwear was quite modest in the twenties. Draw an appropriate bathing suit for a woman or a man during this period. Add something special to make it stand out (seashells, sequins, etc.).

Elsewhere . . .

This chronology gives a few of the important events around the globe during the 1920s. Have students research further any people and events that interest them.

1920
- Mohandas Gandhi reorganizes the Indian National Congress Party. Through peaceful protests he strives to free India from British rule.
- Civil War flares up in Ireland.
- Austrian Sigmund Freud publishes a book about his theory of psychoanalysis.
- Adolph Hitler forms the Nazi Party.
- Palestine becomes a British mandate.

1921
- New Zealand becomes a member of the League of Nations.
- In China, Mao Tse Tung helps form the Chinese Communist Party.
- Ireland is divided. Its south becomes a separate country called the Irish Free State.

1922
- Benito Mussolini becomes the Italian prime minister. Having set up the Fascist Party, he now becomes the country's dictator.
- Egypt becomes an independent country under British influence.
- The tomb of Egyptian Pharaoh Tutankhamen is discoverd by archaeologists Howard Carter and Lord Carnarvon.
- The USSR is formed.
- King Faud I becomes sultan of Egypt.

1923
- Turkey becomes a republic. General Mustafa Kemal, its first president, introduces the Western alphabet to replace Arabic writing.
- An earthquake in Tokyo kills over 130,000 people.
- Two Swedish scientists, von Platen and Munters, design the first electric refrigerator.
- The dictatorship of Primo de Rivera begins in Spain.
- On the art scene, an exhibition of Bauhaus is held.

1924
- The first winter Olympics are held in France.
- Stalin takes control of the USSR and kills millions who oppose his ideas to modernize farming and industry.
- The Ford Motor Company manufactures its ten millionth automobile.

1925
- Hitler's *Mein Kampf* is published.
- Art deco is exhibited in Paris.
- Dr. Howard Carter uncovers the mummified body of Tutankhamen.

1926
- A Norwegian, Rotheim, invents aerosol, which allows liquids to be sprayed in fine mists.
- All union members in England are on strike.
- Panama and the U.S. agree to protect the Panama Canal during wartime.
- In Great Britain, John Logie Baird develops the television.
- A. A. Milne writes *Winnie-the-Pooh*.

1927
- Canberra becomes the federal capital of Australia.
- Chiang Kai-shek takes Shanghai.

1928
- Stalin launches his Five-Year Plan.
- Trotsky is sent into exile.
- Japanese massacre Chinese civilians.
- Mt. Etna erupts in Italy.

1929
- The Serb-Croat-Slovene kingdom becomes known as Yugoslavia.
- The *Graf Zeppelin* makes an around-the-world flight.
- There is Arab-Jewish rioting in Palestine.

62

Politics Around the Globe

Following World War I nations across the globe faced internal conflicts. Read each statement below.
Use history books, time lines of history, and other reference materials to help you identify the country.
Write the name of the country in the space provided.

1._____ 100,000 people die in the Great Kanto earthquake in 1923. Hirohito
becomes emperor in 1926.

2._____ In 1922 it is declared independent of British and French influence. King
Faud I becomes sultan.

3._____ Mussolini bullies his way to power in 1922. The dictator establishes
Fascism there in 1923.

4._____ In 1921 it attacks Turkey but is defeated. Prime Minister Venizelos
brings some stability in 1928.

5._____ An Arab uprising in an African country, begun in 1925, is crushed by
France and Spain the following year.

6._____ Miguel Primo de Rivera seizes control in 1923 and rules as dictator until
his forced resignation in 1930.

7._____ Reza Shah Pahlevi seizes power in 1921 and proclaims himself Shah in
1925.

8._____ In 1927 Chiang Kai-shek ousts the communists and sets up a government
at Nanjing. Civil war follows.

9._____ The Weimar Republic fails to solve the country's economic problems,
and it defaults on its WW I repayments.

10._____ In 1920 it is established as a Jewish state under British administration.
In 1929 there is a major conflict with the Arabs.

11._____ Mustafa Kemal deposes the sultan and creates a modern republic in the
country.

12._____ A general strike among union workers is called in 1926, further crippling
the economy.

13._____ Alexander Karadjordjevic rules over the kindgom of Serbs, Croats, and
Slovenes and renames the country in 1929.

14._____ Civil war erupts in 1920. The following year the country is partitioned
into north and south.

15._____ In 1920 it fails to take the Ukraine. Marshal Jozef Pilsudski establishes a
military dictatorship in 1926.

16._____ This newly-established country is ruled by Thomas Masaryk from 1918
to 1935.

A Treatment for Diabetes

Diabetes mellitus, more commonly known as sugar diabetes, is a disease affecting millions of people worldwide. A person who has this disease is unable to metabolize sugar properly and cannot turn it into energy. Normally, a body derives most of its energy from carbohydrates. Once inside the body carbohydrates are broken down into a simple sugar called glucose, which is converted into energy. Diabetics are unable to complete this process, however, and the result is a buildup of glucose in the bloodstream and urine. Unchecked, diabetes can cause blindness, kidney failure, and heart disease.

Before this century doctors could do little but watch helplessly as their diabetic patients slowly died. Relief was finally provided in 1922 when Frederick Banting, a Canadian orthopedic surgeon, first tested insulin on a human being. Banting grew up in Ontario, Canada, where he was born in 1891. Although his father wanted him to be a minister, Frederick had other plans. After graduation from medical school and serving in the Canadian Army Medical Corps, he set up a practice. To supplement his income he took on a teaching job. While preparing for a lecture on the pancreas, Banting decided he needed more information on the organ. When he realized the connection between the islets of Langerhans in the pancreas and diabetes, he began his experiments with dogs. Using fluids extracted from dogs' pancreatic ducts, Banting and his research partner, Charles Best, were able to create an injection for diabetic dogs. Results were immediate and dramatic. After further testing, insulin was formulated for human beings. In 1923 Frederick Banting was awarded the Nobel Prize in medicine and physiology for this important contribution to mankind.

Suggested Activity

Circle the names of all the foods that are primary sources of carbohydrates.

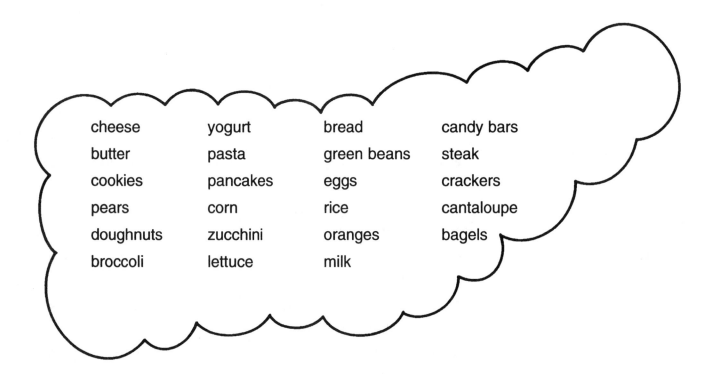

cheese	yogurt	bread	candy bars
butter	pasta	green beans	steak
cookies	pancakes	eggs	crackers
pears	corn	rice	cantaloupe
doughnuts	zucchini	oranges	bagels
broccoli	lettuce	milk	

Gabriela Mistral

Educator, poet, and diplomat are three titles that aptly describe Gabriela Mistral, for she was each of these at different times in her life. An educator first, Gabriela sought solace in writing poetry after an old boyfriend committed suicide. As she became serious about her writing she took a pen name: Gabriela was for the Archangel Gabriel. Mistral was from the cold winds that blow down from the Alps and across the plains of France. While she was able to combine careers in both teaching and poetry writing, Mistral took some thirteen years off from the two to become a diplomat for her country. In all three fields she was an excellent role model for South America.

Gabriela Mistral

Born Lucila Godoy Alcayaga in 1889 in northern Chile, Mistral was raised by her mother and home-educated by her sister, a teacher. Encouraged by her sister, Gabriela went on to become a teacher, too, and taught in rural secondary schools. In 1918 she was appointed director of a secondary school for girls. Before the appointment, though, her first book of poetry had been published to rave reviews. Gabriela continued with her educational career and in 1922 was invited by the Mexican minister of education to help him start educational programs for the poor in his country. That same year her poetry collection titled *Desolación* made its debut.

In 1925 Gabriela began her diplomatic career when she was named the Chilean delegate to the United Nations. From 1926 to 1939 she served as head of the Cultural Committee in Paris. Following this post she worked as the Chilean Consul in Madrid. After being diagnosed with diabetes in 1944, Mistral moved to the United States, where she taught at Barnard college and acted as a cultural attache. There she returned to her writing. Gabriela began to write more poems and also some novels about Chilean life. In 1944 Gabriela Mistral became the first South American writer to win the Nobel Prize for literature.

Suggested Activities

Pen Name Gabriela Mistral was a pen name. With the class, brainstorm a list of other writers who have used pen names. Discuss the purpose of pen names.

Chile Let the students locate Chile on a map. Briefly discuss the culture there.

Research Find out more about this writer's life. Some sources to use include *Herstory* edited by Ruth Ashby and Deborah Gore Ohrn (Viking, 1995), and *100 Women Who Shaped World History* by Gail Meyer Rolka (Bluewood Books, 1994). Compare the accounts of Mistral's life in the two sources. Which facts are different? What might account for these discrepancies?

The Tomb of Tutankhamen

The Egyptians may have been the first archaeologists. They investigated and recorded evidence of their past, including inscriptions hundreds of years old. It would be centuries before some of their own evidences were discovered by others, however. In 1922, after years of searching, British explorer Howard Carter found the burial tomb of Tutankhamen. Nearly 4,000 years old, the tomb was crammed with treasures. It took close to six years to record and preserve the thousands of valuable artifacts that were found there. One room alone contained 171 objects and pieces of furniture.

In the box that follows is a list of some of the objects found in King Tutankhamen's tomb. Find and circle each word in the word search puzzle below.

alabaster	couches	hieroglyphics	scarab	throne
amulets	food	incense	scrolls	vanity boxes
Anubis	funerary bed	mummy	Senet	vases
canopic jars	games	perfume	shabti	
chariots	gold jewelry	sarcophagus	statues	

```
                        A
                     R  S  H
                  S  R  K  F  U
               U  A  N  U  B  I  S
            G  J  A  N  S  O  O  Q  Z
         A  C  R  E  T  S  A  B  A  L  A
      H  I  E  R  O  G  L  Y  P  H  I  C  S
   P  P  V  A  N  I  T  Y  B  O  X  E  S  H  T
O  O  Y  R  L  E  W  E  J  D  L  O  G  B  E  Z  O
C  N  M  Y  U  U  V  N  N  U  I  C  A  A  M  T  H  S  I
R  A  M  B  S  U  S  X  R  I  T  Q  M  R  U  H  F  P  C  H  R
A  C  U  E  S  N  E  C  N  I  B  E  E  A  F  R  S  T  E  L  U  M  A
S  C  M  D  W  X  S  E  U  T  A  T  S  C  R  O  L  L  S  D  F  O  O  D  H
O  K  J  B  Q  Q  A  U  P  P  H  X  R  S  E  N  E  T  Q  C  B  Z  O  W  C  M  C
D  W  N  E  E  X  V  Q  F  Y  S  A  S  I  P  E  E  X  I  Y  M  B  V  S  S  R  J  S  R
```

About Antarctica

Two teams of explorers reached the South Pole in Antarctica in 1912. The group led by Norwegian Roald Amundsen made it there and back safely. A British team headed by Robert Scott did not fare as well. Scott and four others were later found frozen to death in their tent.

Seventeen years later, in 1926, American naval aviator and explorer Richard Byrd flew over the South Pole without incident. Still, it would be some time before various countries (including Japan, the United States, and the former USSR) established year-round research stations on Antarctica.

Find out some interesting facts about this desolate continent by unscrambling the letters within the parentheses and filling in the blanks with the correct words. Then read the paragraphs with a partner.

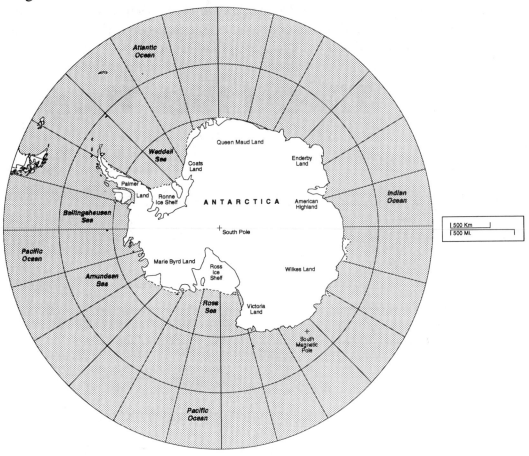

The name Antarctica means "opposite the (critac) 1._____." It is completely surrounded by ocean and remains (cie-vordece) 2._____all year long. Antarctica is the world's (iehstgh) 3._____continent and also the coldest. From mid-March until mid-September there is no sunlight, and the continent is lit by the stars, the moon, and the (otersnhu tislhg) 4._____, or aurora australis. Although it is not home to any native (sumhan) 5._____, Antarctica does harbor some life forms. No trees grow here, but many species of (hecnli) 6._____, moss, and liverworts can be found on its coastal regions. Animal life is also sparse, with some mites and other (sticsen) 7._____which live on the land while seals and (genupisn) 8._____dwell where the land or ice meets the sea.

The First Sighting of Big Foot

According to legends in Tibet and Nepal, there are large, hairy human-like beasts which inhabit the Himalayas. Called *Yetis*, these half-beast, half-human creatures come after children who are disobedient to their parents.

In recent years, large footprints and unusual sightings have led some to believe that such a creature actually exists. For example, in 1921 photographs of mysterious depressions in the snow of the Himalayas led to the first stories about "Big Foot." Through the years the story has been kept alive with other sightings and media attention given to the events. Whether or not Big Foot is a real or imagined creature, or even a Yeti, remains to be seen.

Assignment: You are a news reporter for the *Tibetan High Times* newspaper. A mountain climber has just sighted Big Foot. Write a news story based on the explorer's account. Draw a picture of the creature in the box provided and write an appropriate caption.

Tibetan High Times

(Nepal) _____

_____

_____

_____

_____

_____

_____

_____

_____

_____

References

Yeti: Abominable Snowman of the Himalayas by Elaine Landau (The Millbrook Press, 1993).
Teacher Created Materials #477 *Learning Through Literature—Geography*

An Australian Quiz

When you think of Australia, you probably associate it with Crocodile Dundee, Mad Max, and *The Thorn Birds* because these characters and stories come from Australia. In 1927, when Canberra became the federal capital of Australia, those names were not the household words that they are today. Test your knowledge of Australia with the following quiz.

Read each statement and decide if it is true or false. In the space provided, write **T** if the statement is true or **F** if it is false.

1. _____ Australia is the world's smallest continent.

2. _____ The platypus is a native Australian animal.

3. _____ Spain is larger than the continent of Australia.

4. _____ Australia is smaller than India.

5. _____ The first Europeans to reach Australia were the French.

6. _____ When it was first explored, it was called New South Wales.

7. _____ Captain Cook claimed Australia for England.

8. _____ The British established a penal colony called Botany Bay.

9. _____ Aborigines were the first to settle in Australia.

10. _____ Gold was discovered in Australia in 1851.

11. _____ Eight colonies form the Commonwealth of Australia.

12. _____ The Great Barrier Reef is the world's largest coral reef.

Suggested Activities

Language Write some typical Australian words and phrases on the board, e.g., *sheila* (woman), *tucker* (food), *dinkim* (honest), *bonzer* (great). Discuss them with the class. Assign students to write a creative story, using as many of the words as they can.

Native Animals Australia is home to a number of unique animals, including the cassowary, emu, kangaroo, koala, wombat, bandicoot, echidna, and platypus. Divide the students into groups and assign each a different animal to research. Tell them to find and copy a picture of their animal, along with five interesting facts. Share the completed reports in whole group.

A. A. Milne, Children's Author

Alan Alexander Milne, better known as A. A. Milne, is the author of *Winnie-the-Pooh* stories for children. He was born on January 18, 1882, in London, England, and was the youngest of three boys. An unambitious student, he discovered writing when his brother bet him he couldn't compose a verse as well as he could. But Milne surprised his brother with a well-written poem, and the two collaborated on verse for a couple of years.

After graduating from Trinity College in Cambridge in 1903, Milne became a free-lance journalist. By 1906 he was working at *Punch* magazine as an assistant editor. Seven years later he married Dorothy Daphne de Selincourt. The two had met at her coming-out party and

A. A. Milne

over the years continued to be good friends. During World War I Milne joined the Royal Warwickshire Regiment, a reserve battalion, and served in France. In his spare time he was able to write his first children's book and a play to entertain the troops. When he returned to civilian life he continued with his writing career. On August 21, 1920, his only son, Christopher Robin, was born. Milne wrote poems regularly for *Punch*, and in 1924 a collection of poems, *When We Were Very Young*, was published. It received good reviews both in Britain and in the United States. A second collection of verses, *Now We Are Six*, was published in 1927, but the book that established him as a major children's author was the 1926 story *Winnie-the-Pooh*.

Winnie and Eeyore and Christopher Robin have become some of children's favorite storybook characters. In recent years they were immortalized on screen by the Walt Disney company, which made its first motion picture about Winnie-the-Pooh in 1965. Other animated adventures and some filmstrips have followed, including *Winnie-the-Pooh and the Honey Tree*.

After Milne's death in 1956, his book *The World of Pooh* received the Lewis Carroll Shelf Award. Six years later the same award was presented for his book *The World of Christopher Robin*. Probably Milne's greatest reward was his readers' undying affection for the characters in Pooh Corner.

Suggested Activities

Poetry Read aloud some verse from Milne's *When We Were Very Young* or *Now We Are Six*. Tell the students to think back in time to when they were six years old. Direct them to write a poem about their favorite activity then or an adventure that they remember.

Update With the class brainstorm some adventures that Christopher Robin and Winnie-the-Pooh might have if the story were set in ancient Egypt or in medieval times, for example. Pair the students and have them write a new adventure in a new setting for the two characters.

Volcano!

In 1928 the Mt. Etna volcano erupted, causing widespread damage to the island country of Sicily. It was not the first time Sicilians had faced the destructive forces of this sleeping giant. A major eruption had taken place in 1853, but even more devastating were the occurrences in 1669 and 1169. Over 15,000 people were killed in each of these two instances.

Mt. Etna is neither the largest nor the most destructive volcano the world has ever seen. Read on for a look at some of the world's famous volcanic eruptions. Then research the remaining volcanoes listed on this page and write two or three facts about each in the space provided.

A.D. 79 Mount Vesuvius buried the Roman city of Pompeii under a 20-foot layer of ash.

1883 Krakatau in Indonesia was one of the largest natural explosions in history. The resulting tsunami caused 90% of the more than 36,000 volcano-related deaths.

1902 Mt. Pelee, Martinique, was reponsible for some 29,000 deaths. Remarkably one man, Augusta Ciparis, survived. He was being held in jail, and the walls of his cell protected him.

1985 Nevada del Ruiz in Columbia wasn't a particularly large eruption, but it did trigger a gigantic mudflow. Melting ice and snow killed about 20,000 people.

1815 Mt. Tambora, Indonesia _____

_____

1980 Mt. St. Helens, Washington _____

_____

1983 Kilauea, Hawaii_____

_____

1991 Mt. Pinatubo, Philippines _____

_____

Olympics of the 1920s

Games are the world's greatest sports competition. A tradition begun in ancient Greece in 776 B.C. and abolished in A.D. 394, the games did not begin again until 1896. Since then, the modern Olympiads have undergone numerous changes. Some sports, like rugby, have come and gone while others, like track and field, have remained constant.

During the 1920s there were two important changes in the Olympics. The now familiar Olympic flag first appeared in 1920. In 1924, the first winter Olympic games were held in Chamonix, France. Originally held in the same year as the traditional games, the schedule changed in the 1990s, with the summer and winter games held two years apart.

See if you can learn more 1920s Olympic trivia by filling in the blanks with the correct names. Use the word box to help you.

Sweden	Amsterdam	Germany	Switzerland	Haiti	Finland
England	Paris	Australia	Norway	France	Antarctica

1. The five rings in the Olympic flag stand for five continents: the Americas, Europe, Asia, Africa, and _____.

2. Rugby was last played in the 1924 Olympics when the United States beat _____.

3. Sonja Henie, who was from _____, won Olympic gold medals in figure skating in 1928, 1932, and 1936.

4. Johnny Weissmuller, U.S.A., won three medals in swimming at the 1924 Olympics and two more at _____ in 1928.

5. Eric Liddell's refusal to compete on a Sunday at the 1924 Summer Olympiad in _____ became the basis for the 1981 film *Chariots of Fire*.

6. In 1928 the Winter Olympiad was held in _____, where 500 athletes from 28 countries competed.

7. Paavi Nurmi of _____ planned his races scientifically and held a stopwatch in his hand as he ran!

8. _____ and its World War I allies were not allowed to participate in the 1924 Olympics.

The Discovery of Penicillin

One of the world's most important medical breakthroughs was the discovery of penicillin during the 1920s. Since the 1870s scientists had thought it would be possible to use some microorganisms to kill disease-causing microorganisms, but until Alexander Fleming came along, no one had been able to make the idea work.

Born in 1881 on a farm in Lochfield, Ayrshire, Scotland, Alexander Fleming entered medical school when he was twenty years old. After graduating in 1908 he joined a research group. World War I interrupted his career, yet it influenced his future research. Appalled by the primitive methods of treating war wounds, Fleming determined that once he was back in a lab setting, he would experiment with ways to clean wounds of infectious microorganisms. One method he employed was to grow cultures of a bacteria that caused painful boils. As he later examined one of the containers, he noticed that it was covered with colonies of fuzzy green mold. A second look showed that the mold seemed to be dissolving some of the bacteria. The green fuzzy mold, called penicillium, led to the development of penicillin.

Through a series of controlled experiments, Fleming demonstrated that bacteria could be destroyed by injecting it with fluid filtered from the mold. Because it was so difficult to extract pure antibiotic substance, Fleming's 1928 penicillin research was shelved. Ten years later research was revived by two chemists, Howard Florey and Ernst Chain, at Oxford University in England. The team successfully tested the drug on humans, and by 1943 at least 500,000 people a month were being treated with the antibacterial. In 1945 Florey, Chain, and Fleming received the Nobel Prize for physiology or medicine. Thanks to their careful observations and painstaking work, diseases such as pneumonia and blood poisoning are no longer automatic death sentences for humans. In addition, other diseases, such as strep throat, sexually transmitted diseases, and urinary tract infections can now be easily cured with penicillin derivatives.

Suggested Activity
Grow Mold

Materials: (You will need one of each item listed for each student or group of students.) self-sealing plastic bag, black marking pen, slice of white bread, ½ teaspoon (2.5 mL) of water

Procedure:
- Tell students to label their bags with their names.
- Place the bread inside the bag.
- Pour the water into the bag and seal.
- Place the bag in a warm, dark place.
- Make written observations every day for five days.

Extensions: Experiment with the variables. For example, have some students use wheat bread or place some bags in a refrigerator to see what happens. For more experiments on growing mold, see *Janice Van Cleeve's Biology for Every Kid* by Janice Van Cleeve (John Wiley & Sons, Inc., 1990).

Communism and Fascism

After the Russian people tired of fighting with the Allies in World War I, they turned to solving problems at home. In order to get rid of the tsar and to end the huge gap between rich and poor, they staged a freedom revolution. Instead of the democracy they were trying to create, they got a dictator, Vladimir Lenin. When Lenin died in 1924, he was succeeded by Joseph Stalin. These leaders brought totalitarianism to Russia and an economic system called Communism.

About this same time Italy, too, was undergoing internal strife. World War I had left it heavily in debt, and there was widespread unemployment and inflation. The government, a constitutional monarchy, seemed helpless to meet the pressing needs of the people. Benito Mussolini, the son of a blacksmith, rose to power with his violent anticommunist campaign. Once he was in office, he destroyed democracy in Italy and set up a Fascist dictatorship.

Although communism and fascism are alike in some respects, like maintaining dictatorships by force, there are many differences between the two systems of government. In fact, Fascism grew out of strong anticommunist beliefs.

Use the information in the box below to correctly fill in the chart and compare Communism and Fascism.

1. based on a capitalist economy	4. anticommunist
2. promises eventual release of government control	5. appeals to middle and upper classes
3. seeks international revolution	6. promises a classless society

	Communism	Fascism
a.	appeals to working class and peasants	_____
b.	based on a socialist economy	_____
c.	_____	is extremely nationalistic
d.	antifascist	_____
e.	_____	wants to preserve existing classes
f.	_____	intends for government control to be permanent

74

Stalin's Five-Year Plan

Read the following paragraphs about Stalin's economic plans for Russia. Use the lines provided and the back of this paper, if necessary, to answer the questions that follow.

After Lenin died in 1924, a power struggle developed between Leon Trotsky and Joseph Stalin, two high officials of the Communist Party. The two factions fought bitterly for four years. In the end, Stalin emerged victorious, and Trotsky went into exile. Stalin soon announced the end of Lenin's economic plan and instituted a master plan of economic growth. Called the Five-Year Plan, it established industrial, agricultural, and social goals for the next five years. (In all, there were three five-year plans, but only the first one, instituted during the twenties, will be discussed here.)

Targets were set for industry to achieve. Factories were required to meet huge production quotas, or else the workers and those in charge were punished. This led some factory managers to exaggerate their production figures. The rapid industrialization also brought about some problems for Soviet citizens. Many people were forced to move to new cities where living conditions were appalling. Although the output of capital goods rose by almost thirteen times its starting point, the production of consumer goods increased by only four times.

As for agriculture, the Five-Year Plan changed the organization of Soviet farming to collective farms (*kolkhozy*) or state farms (*sovkhozy*). On a collective farm, the peasants turned over all their land and resources to a collective in return for a share of the profits. On a state farm, all land and goods were owned by the state and laborers worked for wages. At first the Soviet government had to force the peasants into collective farms—some were shot, some starved to death, and others were deported to remote labor camps in the USSR. Overall, the policy was an economic failure and disastrous in human terms.

QUESTIONS

1. You are a farmer in 1928 Russia. If you were given the choice between a *kolkhozy* and a *sovkhozy,* which would you choose? Explain your answer. _____

_____

_____

_____

2. Why do you think the Five-Year Plan was a failure in human terms?_____

_____

_____

_____

Modern Art

On this page you will meet two influential artists of the first half of the twentieth century. Both developed innovative methods of artistic expression and are still popular today. Try your hand at their methods with the suggested art projects.

Pablo Picasso (1881–1973, Spain)

The son of a mediocre painter, Pablo Picasso could draw before he could talk. By the time he was sixteen he had mastered the art of drawing. He shocked the world with his unorthodox styles, especially Cubism. This major artistic breakthrough shattered all former rules of artistic convention. Vital until his death at age 91, Picasso produced an estimated 50,000 pieces of art.

Picasso Portraits

Materials: black and colored crayons, white construction paper

Directions:

- With the black crayon draw an oval which fills up most of the space on the paper.
- Draw a right or left profile down the middle of the face (see diagram).
- On one side draw a front view of an eye, on the other draw a side view of an eye.
- Draw a mouth, hair, and other facial features.
- Color in the facial features, using different colors on each side.

Piet Mondrian (1872–1944, Holland)

Mondrian is most famous for the patterns he created from lines, rectangles, and squares. After studying art in Paris, he stopped painting recognizable figures and landscapes and tried new ways to express his thoughts. During the 1920s he employed three basic units in his work: the straight line, the right angle, and the use of the three primary colors (red, yellow, blue) and three noncolors (white, black, gray). Although he died in 1944, Mondrian's style can be seen in furniture and architecture today.

Mondrian Moods

Materials: ruler; black marking pen; red, blue and yellow colored pencils; white drawing paper

Directions: Use the ruler and black marking pen to draw a series of horizontal and vertical lines on the paper. Vary the thickness of the lines for a more interesting piece.

Fill in some of the resulting rectangles with red, blue, and yellow colored pencils.

     76

Writing History

Transport yourself back in time and imagine the sights, feelings, and sounds of the events below. Choose one situation to write about.

1. After years of fruitless searching, Howard Carter and his men have just entered the first room of King Tutankhamen's tomb. It contains over 150 objects and pieces of furniture. Write a conversation Carter might have had with the head member of his crew as they surveyed the room for the first time.

2. You are visiting Antarctica and have just seen the *aurora australis*, or southerns lights, for the first time. Write a diary entry to explain your feelings as you viewed this magnificent phenomenon or write a poem about the experience.

3. While you are climbing the mountains of Tibet, you spy a half-man, half-beast running in the distance. You're sure it's Big Foot! Write a postcard to a friend back home, describing Big Foot and explaining the sight.

4. It is 1928 and you are living near Mt. Etna in Sicily. Suddenly, the volcano begins to erupt! Make a list of 20 things you heard people say as they tried to escape the deadly force.

5. John Logie Baird of Britain has just invented the television and you are one of the first persons to see it demonstrated. You represent an investment group. Write a letter convincing the group that television will be the next important medium. Explain how it will affect communication and education.

6. It is 1924, and you are a newspaper correspondent in France attending the first-ever winter Olympics. Ski jumping and figure skating are two of the events. Write a news article about the events during one of those competitions.

7. When Lucila Godoy Alcayaga began writing poetry, she chose Gabriela Mistral as her pen name, Gabriela for the Archangel Gabriel and Mistral for the winds across southern France. Choose a pen name for yourself and explain your sources.

8. As dicator, Joseph Stalin initiated a Five-Year Plan to bring his country's economy in line with the advanced countries. You are Stalin's speech writer. Write a speech he will deliver to his countrymen to convince them that such drastic measures are necessary. Include explanations of the consequences of not cooperating.

9. You are Christopher Robin, A. A. Milne's only son, and the basis for the character of the same name in the *Winnie-the-Pooh* books. Write a letter to your father, telling him why you like or dislike being the subject of his books. Tell him if it has been mostly a positive or a negative experience.

10. It is a Sunday at the Olympics, and you are scheduled to compete. You are favored to win, but your religion forbids you to do anything except worship on the Sabbath. What do you do? Write a plan of action you have that would satisfy all those involved.

Names to Know

How well do you know the international figures of the 1920s? Find out with the matching exercise below. Write the letter of the correct phrase in Column B next to the matching name in Column A.

Column A

1. _____ Benito Mussolini
2. _____ Frederick Banting
3. _____ Gabriela Mistral
4. _____ Joseph Stalin
5. _____ A. A. Milne
6. _____ John Logie Baird
7. _____ Howard Carter
8. _____ Vladimir Lenin
9. _____ Walter Gropius
10. _____ Alexander Fleming
11. _____ Adolf Hitler
12. _____ Sonia Henie
13. _____ Coco Chanel
14. _____ Yehudi Menuhin
15. _____ Count Graf von Zeppelin
16. _____ George Mallory
17. _____ Mustafa Kemal
18. _____ Miguel Primo de Rivera
19. _____ James Joyce
20. _____ Leon Trotsky
21. _____ Pablo Picasso
22. _____ King George II
23. _____ Henri Matisse
24. _____ Mohandas Gandhi
25. _____ Alexander I

Column B

A. inventor of television

B. first head of state in the USSR after the Revolution

C. king of Yugoslavia

D. founder of the German Bauhaus design school

E. in protest, fasted 21 days

F. child prodigy violinist

G. tried to climb Mt. Everest

H. Paris designer

I. crossed Atlantic in airship

J. seized control of Spain in 1923

K. Spanish Cubist artist

L. founder of Fascism in Italy

M. wrote *Mein Kampf*

N. deposed by Greek army

O. *Winnie-the-Pooh* author

P. author of *Ulysses*

Q. discoverer of penicillin

R. French impressionist artist

S. archaeologist who discovered King Tut's tomb

T. "Norwegian doll"

U. instituted the Five-Year Plan

V. discovered insulin

W. founded Communism in Russia

X. established the modern Turkish Republic

Y. Chilean poet

Passages

Some later, well-known figures were born during the twenties while idols of another time—and even a few from the Roaring Twenties—died in this same period. Read about them below. See what else you can find out about a particular person who interests you.

Births

1920

- Author Isaac Asimov was born on January 2. A prolific writer, he was known for his science-fiction books.
- Eugenie Clark was born on May 4. She spent her life studying sharks and was known as the Shark Lady.

1924

- Shirley Chisholm, the first African American woman elected to Congress, was born on November 30.

1925

- Maria Tallchief, the first internationally recognized Native American ballerina, was born on January 25.
- The first female prime minister of Great Britain, Margaret Thatcher, was born on October 13. Elected in 1979, Ms. Thatcher remained in office until 1990, when she resigned.

1929

- Civil rights leader Martin Luther King, Jr. was born on January 15. A minister and charismatic public speaker, he advocated nonviolent protest.
- Anne Frank was born on June 12. Her diary account of her life spent hiding from the Nazis made her famous posthumously.

Deaths

1921

- Enrico Caruso was a famous Italian operatic tenor. His recordings brought him worldwide fame.

1922

- Newspaper reporter Nellie Bly, who was famous for traveling around the world in 72 days.

1923

- Wilhelm Roentgen, the German scientist who received a Nobel Prize for Physics for his discovery of x-rays.
- President Harding died while on a cross-country tour.

1924

- Ex-President Woodrow Wilson died after a lengthy illness. In 1920 he was awarded the Nobel Peace Prize.
- Vladimir Lenin, Russia's leader, led the successful revolution that brought the Communist government to power.

1925

- William Jennings Bryan an unsuccessful candidate for president in three elections and prosecutor at the Scopes Trial in 1925.

1926

- Rudolph Valentino was a romantic star of the silent screen. One of his most famous and popular roles was in *The Sheik.*
- Famed magician and escapologist Harry Houdini died of a burst appendix.
- American impressionist painter Mary Cassatt studied and painted mostly in France.

1928

- On December 14, 1911, Norwegian explorer Roald Amundsen was the first man to reach the South Pole.

Then and Now Activities

Make an enlarged copy of the chart on page 81 on the bulletin board or chalkboard or make an overhead transparency. Ask students to add other names and facts from their reading. Make a copy of page 82 for each pair of students and direct them to complete the chart for the current decade. Use the completed work sheets to compare the 1920s and the current decade. Expand the lesson with the following activities.

1. **Word Problems** Compose math problems, using information from the charts; for example, what is the difference between the price of a gallon of milk today and its price in the twenties? Find the percentage increase in the price of milk from the 20s to the current year. Assuming a person worked a 40-hour week, 50 weeks per year, how much money did the average person earn per hour in the twenties? Compare that to the current minimum wage. Have students complete the prepared work sheet on page 84.

2. **Polls** Conduct a student poll to find out which popular 20s books the students have read or which 20s movies they have heard of or seen. Assign students to make a line graph of the resulting data.

3. **Author, Author** Ernest Hemingway and F. Scott Fitzgerald are widely acclaimed authors. Their works have garnered numerous awards and been made into several movies. Much has been written about these two writers. Let students find out some of the fascinating facts about their lives. Compile these facts onto a large chart.

4. **Remakes** Many movies of the 1920s like *Ben Hur, Treasure Island,* and *The Jazz Singer* have been redone more than once. Have groups of students compare a twenties movie with its remake years later by constructing a chart showing the year in which each was made, the stars of each, and whether it was filmed in color or black and white.

5. **Stars** The twenties produced the first movie stars. Learn about some of these early stars and how they influenced future generations. For example, because of what happened to child star Jackie Coogan, laws were enacted to protect the earnings of children. Have students research some of these actors and give a brief report to the rest of the class.

6. **Innovations** By the end of the twenties almost every household had a car. The first TV tubes were being introduced, but it would be another twenty years before television sets became a common household appliances. With the students discuss how the automobile and the television changed the life of the average American.

7. **Crazes** Every era produces its own crazes. In the twenties marathon dances, the Charleston, and mah jongg were popular. Teach students how to play mah-jongg or invite a guest speaker to tell them about the game. Learn to dance the Charleston. Crossword puzzles were beginning to appear in newspapers, and everybody was solving them. Have students work the 1920s Famous People Crossword Puzzle on page 85.

The United States in 1920

Population	121,767,000 (in 1929)
Price of one gallon of milk	$.58
Average annual income	$1,574
Popular books	*A Farewell to Arms*, Ernest Hemingway; *The Bridge of San Luis Rey*, Thornton Wilder; *The Great Gatsby*, F. Scott Fitzgerald
Popular children's books	*Tom Swift* series; *Ruth Fielding* series; *The Velveteen Rabbit*, Margery Williams; *Winnie-the-Pooh*, A. A. Milne; *Bambi*, Felix Salten; *The Story of Dr. Doolittle*, Hugh Lofting
Children's toys	baby dolls that say mama, paper dolls, teddy bears, scooters, wagons, metal trucks, Tinker Toys, Erector sets
Best movies	*Treasure Island* (1920), *Ben Hur* (1926), *The Broadway Melody* (1929)
Favorite actors	Mary Pickford, Greta Garbo, Lillian Gish, Gloria Swanson, Al Jolson, Jackie Coogan, Douglas Fairbanks, Lon Chaney, Rudolph Valentino, Rin Tin Tin, Laurel and Hardy
Styles	bobs, short hemlines, cloche hats, knickers, Lindbergh leather jackets and caps, raccoon coats
Favorite sports	tennis, golf
Sports heroes	Dizzy Dean, Lou Gehrig, Babe Didrikson, Jack Dempsey, Gene Tunney, Sonja Henie, Johnny Weissmuller, Bobby Jones, Helen Wills, Bill Tilden
Famous politicians	William Jennings Bryan, Al Smith
Famous women	Amelia Earhart, Jeanette Rankin, Carrie Chapman Catt, Gertrude Stein, Zora Neale Hurston, Gertrude Ederle, Annie Oakley, Dr. Florence Sabin, Bessie Smith, Bessie Coleman
Famous outlaws	Al Capone, Bugs Moran, Leopold and Loeb
Other famous people	Albert Einstein, Charles Atlas, Alexander Fleming, Harry Houdini, Countee Cullen, Duke Ellington, Aaron Copland, Will Rogers
Crazes	Mah-jongg, marathon dances, the Charleston, flagpole sitting, King Tut, ouija boards, crossword puzzles
Favorite cartoon characters	Felix the Cat, Mickey Mouse, Little Orphan Annie, the Katzenjammer Kids
Popular sayings	*You're the cat's meow* (you look great). *He's a flat tire* (he's boring).
Popular children's games	marbles, the statue game, jump rope, roller skates
Favorite songs	"Yes Sir, That's My Baby"; "Five Foot Two, Eyes of Blue"; "Sweet Georgia Brown"; "Ain't We Got Fun"; "Does the Spearmint Lose Its Flavor on the Bedpost Overnight?"
New foods	Welch's grape jelly; Eskimo Pie; Wrigley's chewing gum
Other innovations	TV tube, model A Ford, moving pictures with sound, cartoon features, zippers, Band-Aids, Kleenex

Then and Now Work Sheet

With your partner fill in the blanks on this page. Compare your answers with page 81.

U.S. Now _____
(*year*)

Population _____

Price of one gallon of milk _____

Average annual income _____

Popular books _____

Popular children's books _____

Children's toys _____

Best movies _____

Favorite actors _____

Styles _____

Favorite sports _____

Sports heroes _____

Famous politicians _____

Famous women _____

Famous outlaws _____

Other famous people _____

Crazes _____

Favorite cartoon characters _____

Popular sayings _____

Popular children's games _____

Favorite songs _____

New foods _____

Other innovations _____

82

Famous Firsts

The box below lists a number of famous firsts in the 1920s. Choose any five and write one on each line below. In the first space after each item, explain how it improved the quality of life in the 1920s. Use the second space to tell how your life today would be different without that item.

- first electric pop-up toaster
- first permanent wave for hair
- Scotch tape
- first contact lens for eyes

- first radio broadcast
- electric razor patented
- dry ice invented
- transatlantic radio telephone

- antitoxin for scarlet fever
- first motion picture
- first successful liquid-fueled rocket
- hair dryer

- potato chips manufactured
- frozen vegetables introduced

Choice

1920s Quality of Life

Life Today

1.

2.

3.

4.

5.

Then and Now Math

Use this page as a whole group lesson (make a transparency for the overhead projector) or cut apart the sections and give one to each group of students. After completion have each group share their project with the rest of the class. This page can also be used as a week-long homework assignment.

1. Find an almanac for the current year and fill in the blanks below with the correct figures. Then figure out the percentage increase in each price since the 1920s (you may use a calculator for figuring this out).

1920s	Now	% Increase
average income $1,574	_____	_____
average price of a three-bedroom house $4,825	_____	_____
price of a new Ford $695	_____	_____
one gallon of gasoline $.21	_____	_____
one loaf of bread $.09	_____	_____
one gallon of milk $.58	_____	_____

2. Below is a chart of prices for popular toys in 1927. Get a catalog from a major department store and find today's prices for comparable toys. Write the current prices on the chart. Find out the difference between the 1920s prices and current ones; write your answers in the proper spaces.

Toy	1920s Price	Price Now	Difference
a red wagon	$5.98	_____	_____
teddy bear	$2.50	_____	_____
sled	$1.39	_____	_____
checkers game	$.39	_____	_____
four-pound metal truck	$1.00	_____	_____
Tinker Toys	$.63	_____	_____
doll that cries	$3.50	_____	_____
Erector set	$1.00	_____	_____

3. Candy prices were considerably lower in the 1920s. For a penny you could buy any of the following: licorice sticks, lollipops, Tootsie Rolls, flat taffy bars, or a jawbreaker. Five cents could buy you any of the following: a Mars bar, Milky Way bar, Hershey bar, pack of Wrigley's chewing gum, Mounds bar, Butterfinger, a Popsicle, or an Eskimo Pie. Suppose you had $.75 to spend on treats. In the space below make a list of five different combinations of treats you could buy for that seventy-five cents in the 1920s.

a. _____

b. _____

c. _____

d. _____

e. _____

1920s Famous People Crossword Puzzle

Read the trio of clues for each person below and write the person's last name in the corresponding blanks in the crossword puzzle.

Clues Across

2. astronomer, cataloged stars, 1924

3. Italian-American, *The Sheik,* romantic hero

6. transatlantic, *Spirit of St. Louis,* hero

8. jazz, African American, trumpet

9. African American, writer, female

11. women's rights, birth control, clinics

13. tennis, female, 1923 U. S. Open

14. *The Great Gatsby*, male, Zelda

15. singer, African American, blues

Clues Down

1. silent films, *The Kid*, first superstar

2. pilot, African American, female

4. poet, *The Dreamkeeper*, African American

5. composer, *Rhapsody in Blue, Porgy and Bess*

7. sculptor, immigrant, Mt. Rushmore

10. English Channel, female, swimmer

12. Sultan of Swat, Yankees, 60 home runs

Looking Forward

From the beginning of the twenties until the latter part of 1929, there was a gradual progression of economic prosperity. People seemed intent on having a good time despite the laws of Prohibition. Speakeasies catered to those who still wanted to drink alcohol. Women demanded more rights, and they got the vote, learned to drive cars, and danced the Charleston. Businesses were booming, and everyone was trying to get rich by investing in the soaring stock market.

The crash in October of 1929 brought the good times to an abrupt end. Many people lost all their money, their jobs, and even their homes as the economy sank into an all-time low. Banks closed, and more and more businesses failed, leaving over 12 million jobless by 1932. The Great Depression affected all people, rich and poor, and lasted throughout the 1930s. The causes of the depression were far deeper than the collapse of the stock market. Perhaps the hardest hit were the farmers, who had not prospered with the rest of the nation during the twenties. By the thirties their situation was even worse. Crop prices remained low, sometimes below what it cost to grow them. Droughts turned their farmlands into deserts, and dust storms plagued the Great Plains. In the cities Hoovervilles were popping up all over. These shanty towns were shacks built of old boxes and boards. One million people occupied them by 1933.

President Hoover believed the depression was over and declared that no government money should be spent on relief programs. Volunteerism was what this country needed, or so he thought. But individuals were already helping one another. It was time for a change.

The changes came in the form of the new President elected in 1932 —Franklin Delano Roosevelt. He built his platform around giving the American people a new deal. Acting quickly, the government established a number of programs to help the citizens. They included the following:

- The Securities and Exchange Commission (SEC) regulated the stock market.
- The Federal Deposit Insurance Corporation (FDIC) insured bank deposits.
- The Civilian Conservation Corps (CCC) employed 2 million out-of-work young men in the nation's parks.
- Social Security established old age pensions, unemployment benefits, and welfare benefits for the elderly, children, and handicapped.

With these and other programs underway, the U. S. was on the economic mend.

Suggested Activities

Insurance. Most banks are now FDIC insured. Assign students to visit a local bank and look for the FDIC logo on the bank's doors. Discuss in class: What does the logo look like and what does it say? What does FDIC insured mean for the banking customer? What is the upper dollar limit on the insurance?

Social Security By the 1990s, many people began to fear that Social Security would be bankrupt within ten to twenty years. Have the students research and discuss what problems the Social Security system faced in that time period. What are some possible solutions for this problem? What is currently going on with the Social Security program?

Literature Connections

One surefire way to interest students in a specific topic is through the use of children's literature. All of the books cited on this and the next two pages are so interesting that they will naturally lend themselves to discussion and further explorations of the subject. Read through the annotated bibliographies to help you decide which pieces of literature you might like to use with your class.

Helpful suggestions for extending these books follow each description.

Ticket to the Twenties by Mary Blocksma

Clothing, entertainment, fads, women, sports, and family life are just a few of the topics presented in this fascinating look at daily life in the 1920s. Pictures, time lines, and firsts add greatly to the interest factor. This book should stimulate a number of questions which will lead to individual research projects.

Extensions

Math On page 11 of *Ticket to the Twenties* is a picture chart of some items that cost $1 in the twenties. Have student groups create picture charts of some items that they can buy for $1 today. Compare their charts with the one on page 11.

Styles Look at the pictures and read the descriptions of clothing on pages eight and nine of the text. Compare them to fashions today. Discuss any similarities.

Creative Writing "Jive Talk" on pages 18 and 19 of the text contains a dictionary of popular twenties slang terms.

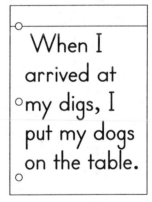

When I arrived at my digs, I put my dogs on the table.

    a. Have students read the list and see if any of the terms are still used today.

    b. Instruct students to choose any five slang terms and write a creative story incorporating all five.

    c. Create a new dictionary of jive talk for all the words listed on pages 18 and 19. Have students come up with current terms for *okay, terrific, nonsense,* etc.

Pastimes Read about family outings, home entertainment, fads, and games of the twenties. a. Compare them to today's pastimes and discuss those entertainments that are still popular. b. Ask students to respond to and complete this statement: *I would/would not like to have lived in the twenties because . . . .*

To Read Children in the twenties had a number of exciting new books to read. Popular titles included *Dr. Doolittle, The Velveteen Rabbit, Winnie-the-Pooh, Bambi, Tom Swift* (series for boys), and *Ruth Fielding* (series for girls). Assign students to read any one of these titles and prepare a short oral summary of the book. Tell them to include an explanation of why they did or did not like the book.

Historical Women Read about the twenties women on pages 52 and 53. List the names on the chalkboard. Assign student pairs to research one: Clara Bow, Coco Chanel, Mary Cassatt, Josephine Baker, Willa Cather, Edna Ferber, Annie Jump Cannon, Margaret Mead.

Teacher's Note: For prepared lessons on Annie Jump Cannon and Margaret Mead, see Teacher Created Materials #493—*Focus on Scientists.*

Literature Connections *(cont.)*

Jump at de Sun. The Story of Zora Neale Hurston by A. P. Porter (Carolrhoda Books, 1992)

Although Zora Neale Hurston wrote numerous books, plays, and articles, not all of them were published during her lifetime. These writings brought her neither the monetary reward nor the fame awarded to some male African Americans of the same time period. Born into poverty in Eatonville, Florida, Zora was shunned by her own father, who had no use for another daughter.

After her mother died, her father remarried, and Zora was left to find her own way in the world. She began writing while supporting herself with a series of menial jobs. Zora studied anthropology under Franz Boaz and combined her interest in folklore with her writing. Zora Neale Hurston died penniless in 1960 and was buried in an unmarked grave.

Extensions

Pre-reading Discuss the title of the book, *Jump at de Sun*. Ask students what they think it means. After reading the book, ask students to explain whether they think it is a fitting title for Zora Neale Hurston's life.

Descriptions With the class, brainstorm a list of words to describe Zora Neale Hurston. Record all responses. Have the students choose three adjectives and find evidence from the biography to support the descriptions.

Twenties Life *Jump at de Sun* offers a glimpse into everyday life for African Americans during the 1920s. Jim Crow laws were used to enforce segregation of African Americans and whites. Describe the conditions prevalent in the South during the twenties. Research what happened to Jim Crow laws and whether any are still in effect.

Plays Zora wanted to present folk tales on stage. "Mule Bone" and "Fast and Furious" were two of her many titles. Group the students and have them write and present a skit about any event in Zora's life.

Spokeswoman Zora Hurston was proud of her heritage in a time when that was not a popular viewpoint, even among her fellow African Americans. Some of her own people found her to be mouthy and controversial. Compare cultural pride in the twenties with cultural pride in the present.

To Read Read Zora's own tale about growing up poor and black in the South during the twenties: *Their Eyes Were Watching God*. A great biography choice is *Sorrow's Kitchen* by Mary E. Lyons (Charles Scribner's Sons, 1990).

War Game by Michael Foreman (Arcade, 1994)

Set in France in 1914, this book tells the story of four English friends who enlist in the army. The boys are sent to the western front and posted as sentries very close to the German trenches. Barbed wire, dead bodies, and devastation surround them, but on Christmas Eve an impromptu truce is observed. The armies take turns serenading one another with Christmas carols. On Christmas Day the peace is continued as the men shake hands, bury the dead, and then engage in a soccer game. Days later, however, the fighting resumes.

Extensions

Prequel Read aloud this sobering story as an introduction to the climate of the world just before the twenties begin. Compare it to the atmosphere of the twenties.

Alike Yet Different With the class make a list of all the ways in which the English and the German soldiers were alike; list ways in which they were different. What conclusions can students draw from the two lists?

History Find out more about World War I—how much longer it lasted after this story takes place and which president was in office then.

Literature Connections (cont.)

War Game (cont.)

Beginnings The assassination of an archduke in Sarajevo provided an excuse for the German kaiser to start fighting. What battles were going on in Sarajevo in 1995? What caused them?

Respond Ask students to respond to this statement: *The officers were alarmed at what had happened on Christmas Day. If such friendly relations continued, how could they get the men to fight again? How could the war continue?*

Discussion Billy thought of enlisting as an adventure. Discuss with students: How do you feel about war as an adventure? Would you let your friends talk you into enlisting to fight in a war?

Moonshiner's Son by Carolyn Reeder (Macmillan Publishing Company, 1993)

Tom Higgins is learning to be a moonshiner just like his pa. Prohibition is in full swing, but that does not stop the Higgins' from being the best whiskey makers around. Besides, Tom wants nothing more than to please his father. When Preacher Taylor and his family move into the Virginia Blue Ridge, their lives begin to change. Young Amy Taylor is as intent as her father on ridding the area of the evils of liquor and tries to change Tom's mind about being a moonshiner. Not until a drinking incident causes a tragedy does Tom begin to waver. Both sides of the prohibition issue are represented eloquently in this believable and well-written story.

Extensions

Point of View Tom's mother and two sisters had walked out on him and his father six years earlier. Mrs. Higgins said it was no life for a woman. Ask students if they would have done the same as Mrs. Higgins or if they would have stayed with Tom and his dad.

Setting Establish that the setting of the story is in the Virginia Blue Ridge. Have the students find the area on a map. Direct them to draw the state of Virginia and label the Blue Ridge area; color it blue.

Lies At times it seems like Pa is lying, but he is always able to explain his way out of it. For example, at his trial for moonshining Pa promises the judge that he will not make any more corn liquor. Instead, he goes home and sets up a still to make fruit brandy. Direct the students to find other examples in the story in which Pa displays a clever way with words. Discuss with students whether Pa is basically honest or dishonest.

Writer Paul Anderson is a writer who often visits with Tom, his Pa, and the neighbors. Tell students to pretend that they are Paul Anderson. Have them record the events of a day in the life of a moonshiner. Write it as a newspaper or magazine article and include the five W's (who, what, when, where, and why).

Taking Sides Construct a class chart which shows the two sides of drinking. On one side list all the reasons Pa and Tom give for allowing drinking; on the other side list all the reasons Preacher Taylor has against drinking. Discuss these pros and cons and add some other viewpoints to each side of the chart.

Further Reading Another book on this same topic that students might enjoy is *Bill* by Chap Reaver (Delacorte Press, 1994). This is the story of Jessica Gates, her bootlegging father, and her dog Bill. Set in the backwoods of Kentucky, the story is about Jessica's father being arrested by revenue agents and her efforts to raise money for his bail.

Writing Prompts

The people, places, and events of the twenties can be combined for some interesting creative writing prompts. Sample ideas are presented below, along with different ways to introduce them.

1. Present any of the following situations to the class. Discuss some possible answers. Assign the students to write a response.

2. Make two copies of this page and cut apart the strips. Place all of the paper strips into a bag. Let each student draw one for his/her assignment.

3. Write a different prompt on the board each day. Give students a set time limit to write a response. Call on some students to share their writings.

- Robert Goddard met Charles A. Lindbergh on November 23, 1929. What do you think they talked about? Write a conversation they might have had.

- The stock market crash of 1929 brought an abrupt end to the boom times of the twenties. Describe your life before and after the crash. In diary accounts tell how it affected your family and standard of living.

- Sculptor Gutzon Borglum knew Theodore Roosevelt personally. Both were energetic, outspoken, and lived life on a grand scale. Write a story or tall tale based on either of these two men's true-life adventures.

- You are a teenage girl in the 1920s and all your girlfriends are getting their hair bobbed and wearing short skirts. Your mother forbids you to indulge in these new trends. Write a conversation you might have with your mother, explaining why you should be allowed to participate in these new fashions.

- During Lindbergh's flight across the Atlantic, he sometimes flew along just above the waves. When he spotted a small fishing fleet he circled one boat and shouted out, "Which way to Ireland?" The stunned fisherman offered no reply. If you were that fisherman, what would be your reaction and response?

- One time, pals Zora Neale Hurston and Langston Hughes headed north in her jalopy. They stopped in Macon, Georgia, to listen to Bessie Smith sing. Write a Langston Hughes poem or a Zora Neal Hurston tall tale about Bessie Smith.

- Your father is a moonshiner, and he expects you to follow in his footsteps. At first, you are willing to go along with his wishes, but then something changes your mind. Write a conversation with your dad in which you explain what happened to change your mind.

- In *Giants of Jazz* by Studs Terkel (HarperCollins, 1975), the author states that each jazz singer had his/her own definition of the blues; for example, *"Blues ain't nothin' but a good man feelin' bad." "Blues is the landlord knockin' at the gate." "Blues is a cryin' woman whose man's gone off an' left her."* Write your own definition of the blues.

- Walt Disney wants to create a new cartoon to highlight Mickey Mouse. Write and illustrate a storyboard (cartoon strip) for Mickey's new movie.

Point of View

Life in the twenties was not a carefree, materialistic, or happy time for every person alive then. Most women perceived and lived it differently than did most men. African Americans' viewpoint of life in the 1920s differed from that of other groups. Immigrants, too, had their own set of problems. For each group mentioned below, describe life from their point of view. Take into account some of the concepts and terms listed after each group.

Women

(Nineteenth Amendment, birth control, flappers)

_____

_____

_____

_____

African Americans

(Harlem Renaissance, KKK, separate facilities)

_____

_____

_____

_____

Farmers

(profits, misuse of the soil, the Depression)

_____

_____

_____

_____

Immigrants

(prejudice, racism, 1924 immigration bill)

_____

_____

_____

_____

Buzzwords

Every era has its own special language of words that are born of people, places, events, and new discoveries. Here are some from the 1920s.

Black Tuesday The date was October 19, 1929, the day that over 16 million shares of stocks were sold as a wave of panic swept the stock market.

Bob A type of short hairdo that many women wore, it was considered indecent by the older generation, but young women considered it fashionable.

Bootleggers These were men who made their own illegal liquor or smuggled it in from foreign countries.

Flapper This name was given to the women who defied the morals of the earlier generation and they styled their hair in a bob and wore short skirts and lipstick.

Depression Business activity declines during a depression, and there is much unemployment and economic hardship.

Harlem Renaissance A period of cultural rebirth occurred in the neighborhood of Harlem in New York City.

Isolationists They are people who believe that a nation should stay out of world affairs.

Jazz An original American form of music, based on blues, ragtime, and other popular music, it allows the musicians to improvise, or do their own thing.

Jazz Age F. Scott Fitzgerald used this nickname for the 1920s.

Jive Talk It consisted of slang terms that were commonly used in the twenties; for example, if someone said you were *the bee's knees,* he was paying you a compliment.

Negro League Because African Americans were not allowed to play on the major league baseball teams, they formed their own league in 1920.

Prohibition The Eighteenth Amendment made it illegal to sell liquor anywhere in the United States. All but two states ratified this amendment.

Red Scare This term refers to the anti-communist sentiment that swept the nation in the early 20s.

Roaring Twenties This is another commonly used nickname for the 1920s era.

Sacco and Vanzetti Italian immigrants who were anarchists, they were convicted and executed for murdering a paymaster and his guard at a shoe factory in South Braintree, Massachusetts.

Speakeasies These were illegal drinking places.

Suffragettes Women who organized for the right to vote took their name from the Latin *suffragium*, meaning "vote."

Sultan of Swat This nickname was given to Babe Ruth, baseball's shining star—in one season he hit an unprecedented 60 home runs.

Teapot Dome Scandal Interior Secretary Albert Fall secretly sold rights to government oil lands in Teapot Dome, Wyoming, to individuals and private companies.

Tin Lizzies This was a nickname for the Model T Fords of the twenties.

New to the Twenties

All of the these words were coined during the twenties. Test your knowledge of these terms by taking the quiz that follows.

- hitchhike
- sports page
- banana split
- perm
- gimmick
- Eskimo Pie

- fascist
- broadcast
- luncheonette
- insulin
- beauticians
- gate crasher

- grease monkey
- mad money
- ambivalence
- blue chip
- jive
- jaywalk

- fine tune
- dinette
- license plate
- garbage truck
- I. Q.
- filling station

Read each of the clues below. Decide which word it describes and write the word on the line provided.

1. It's a frozen sandwich made with ice cream and chocolate. _____

2. Use this saved-up cash for anything you please. _____

3. This shows your tendency to be undecided about a matter. _____

4. Today, stylists cut and style your hair. _____

5. This is the name of a test that measures how smart you are. _____

6. This frozen treat combines fruit and ice cream. _____

7. Diabetics are thankful for this discovery. _____

8. It can make your hair curly or wavy. _____

9. This stock term sounds more like an ice cream flavor or poker game tokens. _____

10. Every commercial has one. _____

11. It is a dangerous way to travel. _____

12. This kind does not live in a jungle. _____

13. Cars gas up here. _____

14. This is not a recommended way to cross the street. _____

15. You'll need a radio to hear this. _____

16. It will help you keep current with baseball. _____

17. You may want to eat here. _____

18. If you are one, you believe in a dictatorship. _____

19. You are not invited to the party, but you go anyway. _____

20. The slang talk that is the bee's knees. _____

21. It gets its name from the word dine. _____

22. When you do this, you adjust something down to the last detail. _____

23. You will need this for your car. _____

24. It transports a smelly problem. _____

Software in the Classroom

More and more software is finding its way into the classroom. Many of the multimedia packages allow students to access photos, speeches, film clips, maps, and newspapers of various eras in history. Although a program may not be written specifically for the topic you are studying, existing software may be adapted for your purposes.

Software

American History CD. Multi-Educator

Compton's Encyclopedia of American History. McGraw Hill

The Cruncher. Microsoft Works

Encarta (various editions). Microsoft Home

Ideas That Changed the World. Ice Publishing

Point of View Series 2.0. Scholastic

Presidents: A Picture History of Our Nation. National Geographic

Time Almanac. Compact Publishing

Time Traveler CD! Orange Cherry

Vital Links. (includes videodisc and audio cassette)

Where in America's Past is Carmen Sandiego? Broderbund.

Videodisc

History in Motion. Scholastic

Using the Programs

After the initial excitement caused by a new computer program wears off, you can still motivate students by letting them use the programs in different ways.

1. Print a copy of a time line for 1920 for each group of students. Assign each group a different topic, like women's rights, airplanes, the automobile, etc. Direct the groups to find out about advances of their particular topic that occurred during the 20s. Have them add text and pictures to their time lines.

2. Let each pair of students choose a specific photo from the 1920s that interests them. Have them research the event and write a news story to go with the photo.

3. Not enough computers? Hook your computer up to a TV screen for large-group activities. Let students take turns typing.

Keeping Current

To keep current with the ever-expanding list of available software programs, you may have to turn to a number of sources, including the ones below.

Magazines:

Children's Software Revue, 520 North Adams Street, Ypsilanti, Michigan 48197-2482. (Write for a free sample.)

Instructor and *Learning* (technology review columns and feature articles)

PC Family and *PC Kids* (available at newsstands).

On Line: A database of more than 900 reviews can be accessed through America Online: go to HOMEPC in the newsstand.

Books:

Great Teaching and the One-Computer Classroom (Tom Snyder Productions, Inc., 800-342-0236).

Internet for Kids! by Ted Pederson and Francis Moss (Price Stern Sloan, Inc., 1995). This text includes a parents' and teachers' guide. It explains how to get on the Internet, what you can expect to find, and a glossary of terms.

That's Edutainment! by Eric Brown (Osborne–McGraw, 1995).

Bibliography

Nonfiction

Altman, Susan. *Extraordinary Black Americans: From Colonial to Contemporary Times.* Children's Press, 1989

Ashby, Ruth and Deborah Gore Ohrn, ed. *Herstory: Women Who Changed the World.* Viking, 1995

Blassingame, Wyatt. *The Look-It-Up Book of Presidents.* Random House, 1990

Blocksma, Mary. *Ticket to the Twenties.* Little, Brown and Company, 1993

Burleigh, Robert. *Flight.* Philomel Books, 1991

Davis, Kenneth C. *Don't Know Much About History.* Crown Publishers, Inc., 1990

Dodds, John W. *Everyday Life in Twentieth Century America.* G. P. Putnam's Sons, 1965

Galbraith, John Kenneth. *The Great Crash, 1929.* Houghton, 1988

Glassman, Bruce. *The Crash of '29 and the New Deal.* Silver Burdett, 1986

Grun, Bernard. *The Timetables of History.* Simon & Schuster, 1963

Hakim, Joy. *War, Peace, and All That Jazz.* Oxford University Press, 1995

Harris, Nathaniel. *The Great Depression.* David Charles, 1988

Herald, Jacqueline. *Fashions of a Decade: The 1920s.* Facts on File, 1991

Hughes, Langston. *The Sweet and Sour Animal Book.* Oxford University Press, 1994
The Dream Keeper and Other Poems. Alfred A. Knopf, 1994

Igus, Toyomi. *Book of Black Heroes: Great Women in the Struggle.* Just Us Books, Inc., 1991

Karl, Jean. *America Alive: A History.* Philomel Books, 1994

Kennemer, Phyllis K. *Using Literature to Teach Middle Grades About War.* Oryx Press, 1993

Klingaman, William K. *The Year of the Great Crash.* Harper, 1989

Krull Kathleen. *Lives of the Writers.* Harcourt Brace & Jovanovich Co., 1994

McNeese, Tim. *American Timeline: Entering the 20th Century, 1901–1939.* Milliken Publishing Co., 1986

Meltzer, Milton. *Brother, Can You Spare a Dime? The Great Depression 1929–1933.* Facts on File, 1933

Millchap, Nancy. *The Stock Market Crash of 1992.* New Discovery Books, 1994

Miller, William. *Zora Hurston and the Chinaberry Tree.* Lee & Low Books, 1994

Murphy, Paul. C. *Since 1776: A Year-by-Year Timeline of American History.* Price Stern Sloan, 1988

Rappaport, Doreen. *American Women: Their Lives in Their Words.* HarperTrophy, 1990

Seuling, Barbara. *The Last Cow on the White House Lawn and Other Little-Known Facts About the Presidency.* Doubleday & Co., 1978

Sharman, Margaret. **1920s.** Steck-Vaughan Publishers, 1993

Smith, Carter, ed. *Presidents of a World Power.* The Millbrook Press, 1993

Stein, Conrad R. *The Great Depression.* Children's Press, 1993
The Roaring Twenties. Children's Press, 1994

Stewart, Gail B. *1920s.* Crestwood House, 1989

Tames, Richard. *The 1920s.* Franklin Watts, 1991

Tilton, Rafael. *The Importance of Margaret Mead.* Lucent Books, 1994

Turner, Glennette Tilley. *Take a Walk in Their Shoes.* Puffin Books, 1989

Weitzman, David. *My Backyard History Book.* Little, Brown and Company, 1975

Fiction

Note: Starred (*) titles are Newbery Medal Books for the year published.

Chrisman, Arthur. **Shen of the Sea.* Dutton, 1926

Finger, Charles. **Tales from Silver Lands.* Doubleday, 1925

Fitzgerald, F. Scott. *The Great Gatsby.* Scribner's, 1925

Hawes, Charles. **The Dark Frigate.* Atlantic/Little, 1924

Hemingway, Ernest. *A Farewell to Arms.* Scribner's, 1929

James, Will. **Smoky, the Cowhorse.* Scribner, 1927

Kelly, Eric P. **The Trumpeter of Krakow.* Macmillan, 1929

Lofting, Hugh. **The Voyages of Doctor Dolittle.* Lippincott, 1923

Milne, A. A. *Winnie-the-Pooh.* (several publishers available)

Mukerji, Dhan. **Gay Neck, the Story of a Pigeon.* Dutton, 1928

Peck, Robert Newton. *Arly.* Walker and Company, 1989

Wong, Jade Snow. *Fifth Chinese Daughter.* University of Washington Press, 1945

Magazines

Cobblestone: "Famous Dates," January 1995; "Prohibition," October 1993; "The Harlem Renaissance", 1991; "The Great Depression," 1984; "The Jazz Sensation," October 1983;

Instructor January/February 1995

Music

Be a Friend: The Story of African American Music in Song, Words, and Pictures. Zino Press. Book and cassette with chapters on jazz and blues. For information call 1-800-356-2303.

Teacher Created Materials

#232 *Thematic Unit—Inventions*
#281 *Thematic Unit—Flight*
#480 *American History Simulations*
#493 *Focus on Scientists*
#496 *Focus on Inventors*
#582 *Thematic Unit—U. S. Constitution*

Answer Key

Page 27

Page 29
1. market in which stocks go down in value
2. person who sells stocks
3. a percentage of profits from a company paid to stockbrokers
4. place where stocks are bought and sold
5. the government agency that regulates stocks and bonds
6. market in which stocks rise in value
7. period of wild selling
8. a share or part in a company
9. buying stock with some money down and borrowing the rest
10. the business of buying stocks and bonds

Page 31
1. 29 4/8 or 29 1/2
2. 54 3/4
3. Bank of America
4. 2,974,000
5. $1.09
6. 9 3/4

Page 59
1. Birdseye
2. Morgan
3. Goddard
4. Dickson
5. Judson
6. Drew
7. Nelson
8. Ford
9. Eastman
10. Disney

Page 63
1. Japan
2. Egypt
3. Italy
4. Greece
5. Morocco
6. Spain
7. Iran
8. China
9. Germany
10. Palestine
11. Turkey
12. Britain
13. Yugoslavia
14. Ireland
15. Poland
16. Czechoslovakia

Page 64
All items should be circled except milk, cheese, butter, eggs, steak, and yogurt.

Page 66

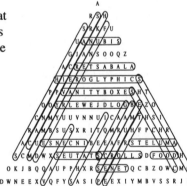

Page 67
1. Arctic
2. ice-covered
3. highest
4. southern lights
5. humans
6. lichen
7. insects
8. penguins

Page 69

1. T		7. T	
2. T		8. T	
3. F		9. T	
4. F		10. T	
5. F		11. F	
6. F		12. T	

Page 72
1. Australia
2. France
3. Norway
4. Amsterdam
5. Paris
6. Switzerland
7. Finland
8. Germany

Page 74

a. 5	d. 4
b. 1	e. 6
c. 3	f. 2

Page 78

1. L	14. F
2. V	15. I
3. Y	16. G
4. U	17. X
5. O	18. J
6. A	19. P
7. S	20. B
8. W	21. K
9. D	22. N
10. Q	23. R
11. M	24. E
12. T	25. C
13. H	

Page 85

[crossword: CANNON, VALENTINO, LINDBERGH, ARMSTRONG, HURSTON, SANGER, WILLS, FITZGERALD, SMITH]

Page 93
1. Eskimo Pie
2. mad money
3. ambivalence
4. beauticians
5. I. Q.
6. banana split
7. insulin
8. perm
9. blue chip
10. gimmick
11. hitchhike
12. grease monkey
13. filling station
14. jaywalk
15. broadcast
16. sports page
17. luncheonette
18. fascist
19. gate crasher
20. jive
21. dinette
22. fine tune
23. license plate
24. garbage truck